SUPER EASY
DUAL ZONE
AIR FRYER COOKBOOK

Many healthy and delightful recipes for beginners, quick to prepare
with British ingredients and European measurements.

Clara Foxley

Table Of Contents

Introduction

In the year 2010, a man Fred van der Weij invented the air fryer. Van der Weij was a Dutch inventor and an entrepreneur. He got the idea from the worldwide famous snack – French fries. He aimed at developing a more nutritious and enjoyable version of this sweet without losing their flavour or consistency. Therefore, it brought about the invention of the air fryer. This clever gadget cooks food using super-heated air and rapid air circulation to achieve crispy exterior and tender interior without any oil.

Air-frying was initially introduced as an alternative way of making healthy French fries and today it has grown into an all-inclusive cooking equipment. This is why we have this cookbook. The Super Easy and Quick Air Fryer Cookbook for Beginners is meant to accompany you on your adventure of trying out different kinds of foods such as appetizers, main course, side dishes, and dessert options.

This is a cook book with easy but delicious recipes fit for beginners which caters for different tastes and diets. Expect classic cravings in addition to unique concoctions for your appetite surprises.

We know that exploring new appliances is a daunting task that requires lots of work. This is why we develop recipes that have brief duration of preparation and cooking. The recipes feature step-by-step directions and easy-to-find ingredients so that you can make tasty dishes which even fussiest of members of the family may appreciate.

So go ahead! Engage the fantastic advantages entailed by air frying such as less fatty foods or meal portions taken, quicker clean-up activity following the cooking procedure, and minimal time consumption. This should be the key that will open up unlimited culinary possibilities to your oven, turning every dish into a specialty.

An Exploration of the Dual Zone Air Fryer's Prominence in the UK

Currently, the market is overwhelmed with the product known as the Ninja Dual Zone Air Fryer which now ranks among the top selling kitchenware in UK in the last few years. For the reason, this dual cooked air fryer is associated with fast and healthier way of cooking which every British household is familiarized by now.

One of the main reasons for the rising popularity of the Ninja Dual Zone Air Fryer has been its ingenious design. It consists of not one but two independent cooking sections where two kinds of delicacies can be cooked with varied settings and temperature. It dismantles the age-old style of cookery that necessitated the simultaneous usage of various devices whose operation could not be coordinated. The Ninja Dual Zone Air Fryer can provide British families with a convenient option of making quick and healthy meals in this rapidly evolving society where the issue of work and life balance becomes more acute by the day.
In addition, some people who care about nutritional concerns are now using air frying while still enjoying their favourite food items. The ninja dual zone air fryer does an excellent job of cooking the food into crisp surface that are usually made with deep fried and less oily. Eating less of the processed and fried products as advised by the NHS Eatwell Guide helps in adopting a healthier lifestyle. Thus, it attracts not only people striving for weight loss but also those who want to eat healthily.

Moreover, flexible cooking settings include air fry, roast, bake, or grill with endless possibilities of dishes to cook. Not only traditional meals like fish and chips or onion bhajis but other ambitious chefs have tried a number of various recipes covering different cuisines for which it provides unvarying outcomes. The ability that makes it compatible with the most number of ingredients across the world strengthens this adaptability and attracts different ethnic groups within the UK.
It is without doubt that accessibility of the appliance has contributed greatly in it take up widely. Cooking novices who in the past would not dare to imagine themselves in the kitchen are now convinced by such simple things in control panels, instructions, and cleaning processes that they can cook. In addition, various companion cookbooks like "SUPER EASY DUAL ZONE AIR FRYER COOKBOOK UK" feature dozens of elaborate recipes that suit both a novice and an expert in cooking. These empower British residents on how to utilize better their Ninja dual zone air fryers.

Lastly, celebrity and influencer endorsements on social media have greatly benefited brands such as Ninja. Air-fried photos and videos are uploaded by food hobbyists on social media platforms such as Instagram, Facebook and TikTok. Such exchanges foster creativity and build a spirit of belongingness among people who have bought a Ninja Dual Zone Air Fryer. Many purchases have been indirectly affected by this digital camaraderie all over Britain as users discover experiences of other users of this gadget.

The Ninja dual zone air fryer illustrates how useful today's technologies can be alongside our enduring tastes for savoury homemade meals. Its prominence within the United Kingdom is attributed to a confluence of factors: innovation in design, healthier choices, flexibility, accessibility, and a strong appeal on social media. It has been a revolution of countless homes with an indelible mark on culinary history.

The Health Benefits of Air Frying

Considering how you will adapt to a healthier lifestyle, modern cooking styles occupy the central place. This is Ninja Dual Zone Air Fryer with top-notch accessories that help to prepare any UK food easily ensuring health benefits for both you and your entire family. In this case, below we discuss the major advantages of the air frying towards a healthier way of living.

1. Reduced Fat and Calorie Intake: Therefore, many people prefer air-frying instead of using other deep-fried techniques because it reduces a lot of calories and fat. Cooking with an air fryer involves using very little oil or none at all and hence, many calories are saved in such cases. Studies have proven that air-frying can reduce up to 80% of fat in your diet. It leads to the loss of fat that helps in improving one's cardiac health, weight management, and overall wellness.

2. Healthier Food Choices: Air frying also prompts healthy food decisions since one can create nutritious foods by testing different ingredients in the appliance. You can be proud of eating vegetables, fish, lean meat and even fruit with the Ninja Dual Zone Air fryer as it guarantees that your tummy gets the deserved satisfaction without being guilty.

3. Preserving Nutrients: Loss of vital nutrients is commonly associated with deep-frying process whereby the food is exposed into hot oil at a very high temperature. These meals are healthy because they involve superhot dry air as opposed to oil which preserves important vitamins and minerals into your body. This helps in ensuring that the flavour and nutrition of the food are kept intact.

4. Reduced Acrylamide Formation: A substance called acrylamide which can be lethal is caused when some cereal based foodstuffs are fried or cook using very high heat. The substance is associated with a number of illnesses such as cancer. Air frying can reduce the development of acrylamide by up to ninety percent which makes it one of the safest ways to cook your favourite dishes.

5. Enhanced Weight Loss Efforts: Air frying helps in losing weight. Additional calories resulting from excessive amount of annealed oil in a traditional fried cooking can be frustrating for losing weight. Air frying offers a way of eating tasty but low-calorie and low-fat foods.

6. Eliminating Trans Fats: Trans fats are largely found in hydrogenated oils, which are commonly used for deep-frying. The elevated level of these dangerous fats boosts unhealthy cholesterol (LDL) while reducing healthy cholesterol (HDL), increasing the tendency to develop heart diseases. Air frying allows one to refrain from ingestion of trans fats, since healthier oils including olive or avocado oil are used as well as cold water misting.

7. Improved Food Safety: It is important to note that high-end models such as the Ninja Dual Zone Air Fryer have multiple safety elements, for instance, the automatic switch-off function, the cool exterior bodies, as well as regulated levels of heating to prevent overcooking or burning of foods.

8. Reduced Kitchen Hazards: Spilling and splatters in oil are more dangerous kitchen hazard than just burning while cooking something in oil. These potential dangers can be eliminated by using air fryer because it does not require a lot of oil.

Speed and Efficiency with Dual Zone

Modern society works at high speed, requiring people to take every second seriously. Therefore, we always try either not to waste or better use our time in order to meet our needs. One of the most alluring features of contemporary household electronics in cooking process is its impact on cooks' speed and productivity in our culinary endeavours. In this regard, the Ninja Dual Zone Air Fryer is uncontested.

The Dual Zone technology is a new concept that makes this multipurpose kitchen gadget more diverse than all other appliances for cooking. Through adopting this high-tech approach, consumers can be able to cook at high speeds with the perfect meal every time.

First of all, we will discuss why dual zone is the most efficient timesaver. Such an air-fried toaster oven is designed with two individually controlled food stations unlike those used in conventional air-fried toasters. The design allows you to cook two types of food at a time, each having different heating levels and cooking times. Instead of frying fish and making baked pastries with other appliances, imagine how you will save a lot of time.

Moreover, this product has high-speed fan that gives rapid and equally flowing hot air hence heat. The meals are evenly cooked, ensuring they maintain the required consistency and texture. No more of the worries that once associated with unevenly cooked portions.

Another time saver that should be mentioned is the match cook. With one button, you can copy any setting from one area to the other. As a result, you will be able to cook different amounts of the same dishes across these two zones without having to worry about any differences in temperatures or cooking times.

Versatile cooking modes of an additional characteristic of Dual Zone technology are also essential for speeding up your cooking process. This has four precise cooking modes that include air fry, air roast, air broil, and dehydrate. For instance, the food will be ready with no heat required prior to cooking it. Whether you want crispy chips or succulent roasts, Ninja Dual Zone Air Fryer lets you master myriad dishes and save time at the same time.

In addition, the SYNCH feature in this appliance is good for large families or crowds. The dedicated service will ensure your food will be ready for serving at the same time hence no delay serving time. Dual zone magic helps you ready main and side dishes simultaneously, serving them all hot at once...fast!

Finally, let us also discuss the role played by the Ninja Dual Zone in simplifying cleaning process. The equipment incorporates non-sticky, dishwasher-friendly removable parts minimizing the process of cleaning. As a result, you save on those precious mins you spend scrubbing your pots and pans, making enough time for you to eat more good food together with friends and family.

Energy Efficiency and Environmental Impact

With climate change being a key agenda now, the green way of life has become a priority to all. There are quite many possible options for this, one of them being decrease of energy consumption on everyday basis. But with the Ninja Dual Zone Air Fryer, we could have the best of both worlds by eating healthily tasty dishes.

Ninja dual zone air fryer has a new innovation that allows cooking two separate dishes with their respective temperatures and settings. Not only does it help save on energy consumption, but it also saves on time. Cooking several dishes together instead of cooking them separately will help you to reduce your electrical bill. Due to this, the air fryer enables environmental conservation by using less energy than other conventional means of preparation.

Energy efficiency is not just about using less energy but also achieving more with every unit of energy that is consumed. Ninja Dual Zone Air Fryer has quick air circulation technology that yields a fast-cooking procedure while still delivering excellent tasting and well-made food items. The modern air fryer is built to distribute the heated air towards a particular direction and cook food in a shorter time span with less fuel.

The other feature that improves the energy efficiency of this device involves an intelligent design for heat management. The heat produced by the Dual Zone Air Fryer is distributed effectively so that your food doesn't have any cold zones. The heat management system is very effective at minimizing energy wastage and yielding high quality results.

In addition, there is less adverse effect on the environment that contributes to the overall lowered energy consumption. Consequently, conventional frying processes emit considerable volumes of carbon dioxide into the air as a result of burning, and thus they contribute in the production of greenhouse gases. However, air frying relies on hot air which is much more environmentally friendly as it leaves less carbon footprint.

Also, VOC chemicals are emitted into the air by traditional cooking methods and they cause environmental harm as well as pose a health hazard for humans. The Ninja Dual Zone Air Fryer however reduces these emissions giving you a healthy cooking environment and less environmental pollution.

So, does waste management contribute positively to environmental protection? Ninja Dual Zone Air Fryer uses minimal oil while cooking and thus, lesser waste of oil is generated. Proper disposal is made easy if oil wastes are reduced since used oil can affect our environment negatively.

The material used in creating the parts and body of the Ninja Dual Zone Air Fryer is also recyclable in an attempt to promote green living. They are also eco-friendly so even after you finally retire your appliance it is still making a positive contribution to help reduce environmental damage.

Setting up the Appliance

In this chapter we help you to set up the Ninja Dial Zone Air Fryer to achieve good cooking results. The features of the air fryer are not limited as it assists in cooking delicious dishes while saving your energy and time.

1. Unboxing Your Ninja Dual Zone Air Fryer: Start off by taking an extra careful approach when you unbox your Ninja Dual Zone Air fryer and then take all the materials that were used for packing it away. Ensure that everything has been put together, including the main gadget, crisp trays, cooking compartments and user guide. Set up the air fryer in a flat and level surface.

2. Inspecting & Cleaning: Do a complete visual check on your air fryer before you use it for the very first time to ensure that there is no broken part and everything is intact. Use damp cloth on the outer body to wipe off dust and debris during the shipment process. One should also ensure they have cleaned all removable parts which are prone to coming into contact with food (crisper trays, cooking baskets) with warm soapy water before their subsequent use. Wash them out in details and let dry before you assemble them into the machine again.

3. Positioning Your Air Fryer: Ensure that your air fryer rests on some heat resistant surface which is sufficiently ventilated and there are free spaces above, around and behind the appliance. It also ensures that the hot air does not rise back inside, causing an excessive heat build-up which could lead to overheating or a fire-hazard.

4. Connecting Your Air Fryer: Plug in your power cord to an electrical outlet which meets your appliance's voltage requisite (usually 110-240 volts). Press the ON button which should be located at the front of the control panel of your air fryer, this will turn the unit on.

5. Familiarise Yourself with The Control Panel: Spend a few moments getting familiar with the controls on your Ninja Dual Zone Air Fryer. In most cases, such a panel normally contains an icon for air fry, roast, dehydrate among other options, adjustable temperature control settings, as well as a timer button. Find out how various buttons work in your instruction manual and instructions on particular cooking modes.

6. Using the Dual Zone Feature: Your ninja dual zone air fryer allows you to cook 2 different meals at a go with the help of separate cooking baskets. For this function you only have to load the ingredients into every basket, and adjust temperature controls as well as time of cooking, respectively. Then you will need to choose the mode of cooking if necessary. They will all finish cooking at exactly the same time, as if they were synchronized in your air fryer.

7. Preheating Your Air Fryer: Achieving uniformity of taste and texture in cooking lies in preheating. Set the air fryer on and select the "air fry" function and then set the temperature control at approximately 200 degrees Celsius or 400 Fahrenheit. Preheat for three to five mins before loading the elements into your air fryer basket.

8. Adjusting Cooking Times & Temperature: Always check your recipe or instruction manual for appropriate cook times and temperatures, depending on different types of food. Some dishes may require to turn or shake it half-way through, in order to obtain uniform cook results.

9. Cool Down & Auto-Shutoff: Ensure that you allow the air fryer to cool off on a heat resistant surface for a few mins after using, before cleaning or storage. Most models have auto shutoff for safety purposes which turns off the appliances after the specified cool down period is over.

10. Bonus Tips: Lastly, a few instant bonus tips that will guide you in optimizing the Ninja dual zone air fryer use.

*   This could include adding just a little oil to some selected ingredients as a means of promoting golden textures and flavours.
*   Experiment with other types of cookware like Silicone or thermal insulated boxes, skewers, and bakeware made especially for air fryers.
*   Please do also be careful to avoid putting too much in your baskets so that the hot air flows evenly around to cook everything properly.

Use and Maintenance

How to Use the Dual Zone Air Fryer

1. Powering On: Ensure that you have plugged in the air fryer and the 'POWER' button. Your air fryer is now ready. It should show a light on display.

2. Setting the Temperature: Press the 'TEMP' button on control panel and enter the required temperate for your foodstuff. Temperature, adjustable in five-degree intervals. Many of these recipes suggest appropriate cooking temperatures.

3. Cooking Time: Press the "TIMER" button to set the cooking period as specified in your recipe. Pressing '+' or '-' will extend or shorten the cooking time by a minute at once. You should ensure that you do not exceed one-hour of cooking in your Ninja Dual Zone Air Fryer.

4. Preheating: Pre-heat is also necessary in some recipes prior to the introduction of food into the air fryer basket; this ensures even cooking. Setting the countdown to three mins while selecting the desired cook setting is sufficient to preheat.

5. Loading Food into Basket(s): After putting on the oven mitts, carefully pull out the air fryer's basket(s) using its handle(s). Arrange one layer of food in each basket to avoid any overcrowding and allow maximum air circulation resulting in uniform baking.

6. Placing Basket(s) inside Air Fryer: Grab the basket handle using the oven mitts and insert it back to its position in the unit. Thereafter, it will be a click-type sound that denotes that the basket is safely locked in place.

7. Cooking: After setting the timer, click 'START/STOP' to begin cooking. Once again, the Ninja dual zone air fryer will do the rest – blowing hot air across your food, just as perfection!

8. Checking Food: Use START/STOP button to temporarily stop cooking when it is necessary for you to check on, shuffle or flip your food. Remember to use oven mitts when doing so.

9. Powering Off: After cooking, press 'power' button for three seconds to turn down the air fryer. Ensure that you always allow the unit to cooling down, disconnecting it once more and then placing it in storage.

Performing Daily Maintenance

To keep your Ninja Dual Zone Air Fryer in tip-top condition, follow these maintenance steps:

1. Disconnect: When cleaning always remember to unplug the air fryer.

2. Rinsing Crumbs from Basket: First remove your basket from the unit and shake them both thoroughly in a bin or tray; so, the unburned food and breadcrumbs will come away easily for a better outcome.

3. Washing Basket(s) and Crisper Plate(s): Gently wash the basket(s) and crisp plates using warm and soapy water either by hand or in a dishwasher if they are dishwasher-friendly. Do not use abrasive cleaners, also use a sponge while doing it because their non-stick coating may be damaged by them.

4. Cleaning Exterior: To deal with splashes of fat and spill over the surface of the appliance use piece or towel dampened with water solution of washing up liquid before rubbing it carefully with dry rag.

5. Ensure Dryness Before Use: Ensure that you allow all components of the air fryer to become completely dry before using it again.

Cleaning Your Dual Zone

Cleanliness is an important aspect that will help prolong the life of your appliance as well as guarantee tasty, food-safe meals. We shall in this chapter discuss how you can clean your air fryer for the highest performance durability.

1. Unplug the air fryer before cleaning: Firstly, ensure you turn off your Ninja Dual Zone Air Fryer from its power point. It makes sure that there is no risk of electrocution when one uses the apparatus for cleaning.

2. Cool down before cleaning: It is important to let an air fryer rest in a safe place for about half an hour after use before attempting to clean it to avoid burns, and other related damages.

3. Clean after each use: Regular cleaning ensures that no foodstuffs are left in the frying chamber, there is no accrual of oil or other contaminants, and bacteria development is prevented on exposed sections.

4. Remove the cooking trays and basket: Unplug all detachable parts of your air fryer like the cooking trays, crisper plate, multi-purpose basket as well as the wire racks. However, these parts can be washed with warm soapy water and nonabrasive sponges/cloth. Do not use rough or sharp scouring agents that can injure the surface of non-sticking material.

5. Use dishwasher-safe parts: Labels such as dishwasher-safe will inform you that those removable components can go straight into your dishwasher without prior hand washing.

6. Wipe down interior surfaces: Clean all inner walls, ceiling and floor of the cooking chamber using a soft sponge or a cloth dipped into warm soapy water. Carefully wash out all particles of food and clean each corner without damaging the inner surface of this vessel. Wash them properly using water then dry up with a clean and soft material.

7. Clean the heating element: Make sure you clean around the heating element placed on top of your Ninja Dual Zone Air Fryer with a dampened microfiber cloth dipped in soapy warm water. The heating element should not be dipped in water or wet. Water damages are irreversible.

8. Clean the exterior: Using wet towel damped in warm, soapy water, clean your air fryer appliance from outside. Wash well and pat dry using a clean cloth.

9. Clean the control panel: Carefully clean the front screen of the Ninja dual zone air fryer, wiping it with a wet towel in which you have dissolved a drop of mild dishwashing liquid. Wet and dry using lint free towel.

10. Reassemble and store air fryer properly: Make sure you clean and dry all parts and completely remove any soap residue before you put them back together following your user manual. When you need to store your Ninja Dual Zone, Air Fryer leave enough space around so that there is free circulation of air to avoid mildew or moulds.

11. Frequent deep cleaning: Clean your air fryer every three times of four months. Descale and degrease the interior surfaces of cooking pot and utensils to avoid contaminants that could affect your food taste and/or safety.

12. Consult your owner's manual: For cleaning and maintenance procedures as well as optimal operation, always consult your Ninja Kitchen owners' manual.

HERE IS YOUR FREE GIFT!

• 30 GLOBAL FLAVOURS RECIPES

• 30-DAY MEAL PLAN

• WEEKLY SHOPPING LIST

SCAN HERE TO DOWNLOAD IT

Classic Full
English Breakfast

🕐 **Prep:** *15* mins   🍱 **Cook:** *13* mins   🍽 **Serves:** *4*

Directions

1. Warm up your Dual Zone air fryer to 180°C in both zones.
2. Put bacon plus sausages in the first zone. Fry within fifteen mins till crispy, turning once.
3. In your second zone, put tomatoes plus mushrooms, then cook within ten mins.
4. Move bacon, sausage, tomatoes, plus mushrooms to your plate, then cover using foil.
5. In your non-stick frying pan on moderate-high temp, add oil, then cook eggs within two mins till whites are set. Flavour it using salt plus pepper.
6. Put cooked eggs plus toasted bread in your prepared plate, then serve.

Ingredients

700 grams thick-cut bacon - 400 grams pork sausages - 300 grams cherry tomatoes, halved - 200 grams button mushrooms, cleaned & halved - Eight big eggs - 200 millilitres vegetable oil, for frying eggs - Sixteen bread slices, toasted - Salt & pepper, as required

NUTRITIONAL VALUES (PER SERVING): CALORIES 153; CARBS 98G; FAT 95G; PROTEIN 68G

Air-Fried
Black Pudding Bites

🕐 **Prep:** *10* mins   🍱 **Cook:** *10* mins   🍽 **Serves:** *4*

Directions

1. Warm up your ninja Dual Zone Air Fryer (first zone) to 200°C.
2. Flavour flour using salt plus pepper in your shallow container. Put beaten eggs in your second container. Put breadcrumbs on your plate.
3. Coat each black pudding cube in seasoned flour, dip them into egg mixture. Roll them in breadcrumbs till coated.
4. Put breaded black pudding bites in your greased cooking basket. Cook within ten mins till crisp, turning once. Serve.

Ingredients

300 grams black pudding, sliced into bite-sized cubes - 100 grams plain flour - Two big eggs, beaten - 150 grams breadcrumbs - 10 millilitres vegetable oil - Salt & pepper, as required

NUTRITIONAL VALUES (PER SERVING): CALORIES 380; CARBS 38G; FAT 16G; PROTEIN 20G

Hash
Brown Perfection

🕐 **Prep:** *15* mins   📟 **Cook:** *20* mins   🍽 **Serves:** *4*

Directions

1. In your big container, mix potatoes plus onion, then squeeze out excess moisture. Flavour it using salt plus pepper, then mix again.
2. Warm up your Ninja Dual Zone Air Fryer to 200°C.
3. Split potato mixture into four, then shape each into a hash brown patty. Move them in your cooking baskets. Spray oil on top.
4. Cook within ten mins, flip them, then cook again within ten mins till crispy. Serve.

Ingredients

600 grams russet potatoes, peeled & shredded - 100 grams onion, finely chopped - 40 millilitres vegetable oil - Two grams salt - One-gram black pepper

NUTRITIONAL VALUES (PER SERVING): CALORIES: 260; CARBS: 34G; FAT: 12G; PROTEIN: 4G

Eggs
Royale Toasties

🕐 **Prep:** *15* mins   📟 **Cook:** *10* mins   🍽 **Serves:** *4*

Directions

1. Warm up your Ninja Dual Zone air fryer to 180°C.
2. Boil your pot within water, then add vinegar. Add eggs, then poach within three mins till whites are set. Strain.
3. Lay out four bread slices, then put smoked salmon across them. Put one poached egg on each salmon.
4. Drizzle each using hollandaise sauce, then add cheddar on top. Close each toastie using another bread slice, then brush them using butter.
5. Put them in your cooking baskets, then cook within five mins till crispy. Remove, cool them down, slice, then serve.

Ingredients

200 grams smoked salmon - Four big eggs - 100 grams cheddar cheese, grated - Eight bread slices - 250 millilitres hollandaise sauce - 50 millilitres white vinegar - 30 grams butter, dissolved

NUTRITIONAL VALUES (PER SERVING): CALORIES: 570; CARBS: 42G; FAT: 33G; PROTEIN: 29G

Morning Mushroom
& Spinach Frittata

🕐 **Prep:** *10 mins*   📠 **Cook:** *15 mins*   🍽 **Serves:** *4*

Directions

1. Warm up your ninja Dual Zone Air Fryer to 180°C.
2. In your container, whisk eggs, milk, salt, plus pepper.
3. Add spinach, mushrooms, onion, plus tomatoes in your greased cooking basket. Pour egg mixture, then sprinkle cheddar cheese on top.
4. Cook within fifteen mins till cooked. Remove, cool it down, then serve.

Ingredients

300 grams baby spinach - 200 grams mushrooms, sliced - 70 grams cherry tomatoes, halved - 100 grams onion, chopped - 150 grams grated cheddar cheese - Eight big eggs - 50 millilitres milk - Salt & pepper, as required

---

NUTRITIONAL VALUES (PER SERVING): CALORIES: 365; CARBS: 11G; FAT: 25G; PROTEIN: 26G

Air-Crisped
Porridge Oats Bars

🕐 **Prep:** *10 mins*   📠 **Cook:** *12 mins*   🍽 **Serves:** *6*

Directions

1. In your big container, mix oats, dried fruit, nuts, cinnamon, and nutmeg. Add the honey, oil, plus vanilla, then mix well.
2. Warm up your ninja Dual Zone air fryer to 180°C. Add oat mixture into your lined cooking basket. Cook within twelve mins till crispy. Remove, cool it down, slice, then serve.

Ingredients

180 grams porridge oats - 75 grams dried fruit - 50 grams chopped nuts - Four grams cinnamon, ground - Two grams nutmeg, ground - 60 millilitres honey - 30 millilitres sunflower oil - Five millilitres vanilla extract

---

NUTRITIONAL VALUES (PER SERVING): CALORIES: 290; CARBS: 37G; FAT: 13G; PROTEIN: 5G

Maple-Glazed
Breakfast Sausages

🕐 Prep: *10* mins   📷 Cook: *12* mins   🔔 Serves: *4*

Directions

1. In your small container, mix maple syrup, mustard, thyme, salt, plus pepper. Put aside.
2. Warm up your ninja Dual Zone Air Fryer to 180°C.
3. Add sausages in your greased basket, then cook within six mins.
4. Remove your basket, then brush sausages using glaze mixture. Cook again within six mins till golden. Serve.

Ingredients

500 grams pork breakfast sausages - 60 millilitres maple syrup - 15 grams mustard, whole grain - Five grams dried thyme - Salt & pepper, as required

NUTRITIONAL VALUES (PER SERVING): CALORIES: 431; CARBS: 16G; FAT: 33G; PROTEIN: 19G

Toasted Granola
Clusters

🕐 Prep: *10* mins   📷 Cook: *20* mins   🔔 Serves: *6*

Directions

1. Warm up your ninja Dual Zone air fryer to 160°C.
2. In your big container, mix oats, nuts, seeds, plus coconut flakes.
3. In your small container, mix maple syrup plus coconut oil. Combine it with oat mixture till blended.
4. Add it to your lined cooking basket (first zone). "Roast" within ten mins. Mix well, then "Roast" again within ten mins till crispy. Remove, then cool it down.
5. Add dried fruit, then mix well. Serve.

Ingredients

300 grams rolled oats - 100 grams mixed nuts, chopped - 50 grams mixed seeds - 40 grams coconut flakes - 60 millilitres maple syrup - 30 millilitres coconut oil, dissolved - Salt, as required - 80 grams dried fruit

NUTRITIONAL VALUES (PER SERVING): CALORIES: 401; CARBS: 48G; FAT: 20G; PROTEIN: 9G

Quick Air-Fried
Bacon Butties

🕐 **Prep:** *10 mins*   📱 **Cook:** *10 mins*   🍽 **Serves:** *2*

Directions

1. Warm up your Ninja Dual Zone Air Fryer to 200°C.
2. Put bacon into your cooking basket (first zone), then cook within eight mins, turning once. Remove, then strain excess oil.
3. In your small container, mix ketchup plus mayonnaise.
4. Spread some sauce on half of each bread roll, then add two bacon slices. Serve.

Ingredients

Four bacon slices
Two bread rolls, halved
20 millilitres ketchup
30 millilitres mayonnaise

NUTRITIONAL VALUES (PER SERVING): CALORIES: 463; CARBS: 46G; FAT: 21G; PROTEIN: 22G

Scotch
Egg Delights

🕐 **Prep:** *20 mins*   📱 **Cook:** *12 mins*   🍽 **Serves:** *4*

Directions

1. Flavour sausage meat using salt plus pepper. Split it into four, then flatten each. Wrap each boiled egg using sausage meat.
2. Put flour, beaten eggs, and breadcrumbs in three separate plates. Roll each wrapped egg in flour, dip into eggs, then coat in breadcrumbs.
3. Warm up your Ninja Dual Zone Air Fryer to 180°C.
4. Put two Scotch eggs in each greased cooking basket, then cook within twelve mins till crispy, turning them once. Serve.

Ingredients

Four big eggs, hard-boiled & peeled - 450 grams
sausage meat - 100 grams flour, all-purpose -
Two big eggs, beaten (for coating) - 150 grams
breadcrumbs - Salt & pepper, as required

NUTRITIONAL VALUES (PER SERVING): CALORIES: 650; CARBS: 40G; FAT: 40G; PROTEIN: 30G

Tomato & Mozzarella
Breakfast Pockets

🕐 **Prep:** *10* mins   📟 **Cook:** *8* mins   🍽 **Serves:** *4*

Directions

1. Warm up your Ninja Dual Zone Air Fryer to 200°C.
2. Put four pastry rectangles on one of your cooking trays. Spoon some mozzarella onto each, then top using cherry tomato.
3. Put egg onto each, then flavour it using salt plus pepper. Top each using a second puff pastry rectangle, then crimp edges to seal. Brush oil on tops.
4. Put them in each zone, then cook within eight mins till golden. Serve.

Ingredients

200 grams puff pastry, rolled out & sliced into eight rectangles - 100 grams cherry tomatoes, halved - 150 grams mozzarella cheese, grated - Four big eggs - 30 millilitres olive oil - Salt & pepper, as required

NUTRITIONAL VALUES (PER SERVING): CALORIES: 630; CARBS: 38G; FAT: 45G; PROTEIN: 23G

Baked Beans
& Toast Cups

🕐 **Prep:** *10* mins   📟 **Cook:** *12* mins   🍽 **Serves:** *4*

Directions

1. Warm up your Ninja Dual Zone Air Fryer to 180°C.
2. In your container, mix beans plus half of cheddar. Put aside.
3. Brush each bread slice using oil. Press each into your cooking basket (first zone), creating cups.
4. Cook within three to four mins till slightly golden. Remove. Put baked bean mixture into your bread cups, then add rest of cheddar.
5. Put filled toast cups into your cooking basket (first zone), then cook within five to six mins. Remove, then flavour it using salt plus pepper. Serve.

Ingredients

400 grams canned baked beans - 80 grams cheddar cheese, grated - Eight bread slices, crusts removed & flattened each - 30 millilitres olive oil - Salt & pepper, as required

NUTRITIONAL VALUES (PER SERVING): CALORIES: 448; CARBS: 53G; FAT: 20G; PROTEIN: 20G

Morning **Blueberry Muffins**

🕐 **Prep:** *10* mins 📠 **Cook:** *15* mins 🍽 **Serves:** *6*

Directions

1. Warm up your ninja Dual Zone Air Fryer to 180°C.
2. In your big container, mix flour, sugar, baking powder, plus salt.
3. In your separate container, mix butter, milk, vanilla, plus egg. Combine it with flour mixture till blended. Fold in blueberries.
4. Pour batter among your six greased muffin cups. Put them into each cooking basket. Cook within fifteen mins till firm. Remove, cool them down, then serve.

Ingredients

150 grams flour, all-purpose - 100 grams sugar, granulated - 50 grams unsalted butter, dissolved - 150 grams fresh blueberries - 125 millilitres milk - Five millilitres vanilla extract - One big egg, beaten - 2.5millilitres baking powder - Salt, as required

NUTRITIONAL VALUES (PER SERVING): CALORIES: 270; CARBS: 41G; FAT: 10G; PROTEIN: 4G

Sizzling **Kippers with Lemon**

🕐 **Prep:** *10* mins 📠 **Cook:** *15* mins 🍽 **Serves:** *4*

Directions

1. Warm up your ninja Dual Zone air fryer to 180°C.
2. Put kippers on your tray, then drizzle using oil. Add zest, then flavour them using pepper plus salt.
3. Put tray into your cooking basket, then cook within ten mins. Pour lemon juice on kippers, then cook within five mins till crispy. Serve.

Ingredients

800 grams kippers
One lemon, zested & halve juiced
40 millilitres olive oil
Five grams black pepper
Five grams sea salt

NUTRITIONAL VALUES (PER SERVING): CALORIES 350; CARBS 1G; FAT 20G; PROTEIN 36G

Welsh
Rarebit Bites

🕐 **Prep:** *10 mins*   📷 **Cook:** *5 mins*   🍽 **Serves:** *2-3*

Directions

1. In you small saucepan, dissolved butter on moderate-low temp. Add flour, then whisk till you have a smooth paste. Slowly add milk, mixing till smooth.
2. Mix in cheese, Worcestershire, mustard, salt, plus pepper. Cook on low temp till smooth. Cool slightly. Spoon it onto each bread.
3. Warm up your Ninja Dual Zone Air Fryer to 200°C.
4. Put Welsh Rarebit Bites into your cooking basket, then cook within five mins till golden. Serve.

Ingredients

200 grams mature cheddar cheese, grated - 100 millilitres milk - 50 grams plain flour - 30 grams butter - Five millilitres Worcestershire sauce - Two millilitres English mustard - One millilitre each salt & black pepper - Six wholegrain bread slices, crusts removed & sliced into squares

NUTRITIONAL VALUES (PER SERVING): CALORIES 430; CARBS 35G; FAT 25G; PROTEIN 20G

Crispy
Haggis Balls

🕐 **Prep:** *15 mins*   📷 **Cook:** *15 mins*   🍽 **Serves:** *4*

Directions

1. Warm up your Ninja Dual Zone Air Fryer to 200°C.
2. Put flour, beaten eggs, and breadcrumbs in three separate shallow containers. Roll each ball in flour, dip it in egg, then coat it using breadcrumbs.
3. Put breaded haggis balls on your both cooking baskets, then spray it using oil. "Air fry" within fifteen mins, till crispy, turning once. Serve.

Ingredients

500 grams haggis, case removed & shape them into small balls - 100 grams flour, all-purpose - Two big eggs, beaten - 150 grams panko breadcrumbs - One-litre sunflower oil

NUTRITIONAL VALUES (PER SERVING): CALORIES 450; CARBS 25G; FAT 26G; PROTEIN 23G

Air-Fried
English Muffin Pizza

🕐 **Prep:** *10 mins*   📷 **Cook:** *8 mins*   🍽 **Serves:** *4*

Directions

1. Warm up your ninja Dual Zone Air Fryer to 180°C.
2. Spread some marinara sauce on each muffin half. Sprinkle 25 grams mozzarella onto each. Add tomatoes plus olives on top.
3. Put four prepared muffin pizza into each cooking basket. Cook within eight mins till cheese is melted. Remove, cool them down, then serve.

Ingredients

Four English muffins, halved - 120 millilitres marinara sauce - 200 grams mozzarella cheese, shredded - 100 grams cherry tomatoes, halved - 50 grams sliced black olives - 30 grams chopped basil

NUTRITIONAL VALUES (PER SERVING): CALORIES: 310; CARBS: 34G; FAT: 14G; PROTEIN: 18G

Spiced Potato
Breakfast Wedges

🕐 **Prep:** *15 mins*   📷 **Cook:** *20 mins*   🍽 **Serves:** *4*

Directions

1. Warm up your ninja Dual Zone Air Fryer to 200°C.
2. In your big container, mix potatoes, oil, paprika, powdered garlic, cayenne, salt, plus pepper.
3. Split seasoned potatoes on both cooking basket, then cook within ten mins. Shake both cooking basket, then cook within ten mins till crispy. Serve.

Ingredients

800 grams potatoes, wedges
30 millilitres olive oil
Ten grams smoked paprika
Eight grams powdered garlic
Five grams cayenne pepper
Salt & black pepper, as required

NUTRITIONAL VALUES (PER SERVING): CALORIES: 260; CARBS: 41G; FAT: 9G; PROTEIN: 6G

Smoked Salmon
& Cream Cheese Bagels

🕐 **Prep:** *10 mins*   📠 **Cook:** *5 mins*   🛎 **Serves:** *4*

Directions

1. Warm up your ninja Dual Zone Air Fryer to 180°C.
2. Put bagel halves in your both cooking basket, then cook within three to five mins till golden. Remove, then cool them slightly.
3. In your small container, mix cream cheese plus lemon juice. Spread some prepared mixture onto each bagel.
4. Put smoked salmon plus cucumber on top. Add capers, pepper, plus dill onto each bagel, then close them using rest of bagel. Serve.

Ingredients

Four plain bagels, sliced each in half - 200 grams smoked salmon - 120 grams cream cheese - 50 grams cucumber - 30 millilitres lemon juice - Eight grams capers, strained - Black pepper, as required - A handful of dill, chopped

NUTRITIONAL VALUES (PER SERVING): CALORIES: 410; CARBS: 45G; FAT: 18G; PROTEIN: 24G

Quick-Fry Crumpets
With Honey Drizzle

🕐 **Prep:** *10 mins*   📠 **Cook:** *8 mins*   🛎 **Serves:** *4*

Directions

1. In your big container, mix flour, baking soda, plus salt.
2. In your separate container, mix milk plus warm water. Add active dry yeast, mixing till dissolved. Let it sit within five mins till frothy.
3. Mix in milk mixture slowly into your flour mixture till smooth. Cover, then let it rest within one hour till doubled in size.
4. Warm up your Ninja Dual Zone Air Fryer to 180°C. Pour four batter portions into each cooking basket.
5. Cook within six mins till slightly crispy. Flip each, then cook within two mins till golden. Remove, then cool them down.
6. Warm up honey in your small saucepan on low temp. Stack crumpets on your plates, then drizzle honey on top. Serve.

Ingredients

200 grams flour, all-purpose - One gram baking soda - Two grams salt - 300 millilitres whole milk - 100 millilitres warm water - Five grams active dry yeast - 20 grams unsalted butter, dissolved - 50 grams honey

NUTRITIONAL VALUES (PER SERVING): CALORIES 382; CARBS 66G; FAT 9G; PROTEIN 11G

Classic
Fish & Chips

🕐 **Prep:** *15 mins*   📱 **Cook:** *20 mins*   🍽 **Serves:** *4*

Directions

1. Warm up your ninja Dual Zone air fryer to 200°C.
2. Flavour fish fillets using salt plus pepper.
3. In your big container, whisk flour plus sparkling water till smooth. Dip each fish fillet into it till coated.
4. Split potatoes plus battered fish in each greased cooking basket. Cook them within ten mins, swap baskets, then cook within ten mins till crisp. Serve.

Ingredients

400 grams white fish fillets, pat dried
800 grams potatoes, peeled & sliced into chips
180 grams flour, all-purpose
240 millilitres sparkling water, chilled
Salt & pepper, as required

NUTRITIONAL VALUES (PER SERVING): CALORIES: 475; CARBS: 61G; FAT: 18G; PROTEIN: 23G

Vegetable
Spring Rolls

🕐 **Prep:** *20 mins*   📱 **Cook:** *10 mins*   🍽 **Serves:** *4*

Directions

1. In your big container, mix vegetables, bean sprouts, rice noodles, soy sauce, hoisin sauce, garlic, ginger, salt plus pepper.
2. Put spring roll wrappers on your clean work surface. Add some vegetable mixture onto each wrapper. Roll it up to seal.
3. Warm up your ninja Dual Zone Air Fryer to 190°C.
4. Put spring rolls in each cooking basket, then cook within ten mins till crispy. Serve.

Ingredients

200 grams julienned mixed vegetables - 100 grams bean sprouts - 50 grams cooked rice noodles - 20 millilitres soy sauce - 10 millilitres hoisin sauce - 10 grams minced garlic - Five grams grated ginger - Salt & pepper, as required - Eight spring roll wrappers - 30 millilitres water

NUTRITIONAL VALUES (PER SERVING): CALORIES: 230; CARBS: 41G; FAT: 3.8G; PROTEIN: 6G

Prawn
Toast Triangles

🕐 **Prep:** *15 mins* 📦 **Cook:** *8 mins* 🍽 **Serves:** *4*

Directions

1. In your food processor, process prawns, water chestnuts, onions, garlic, sesame oil, and soy sauce till smooth.
2. Spread some prawn mixture on each bread triangle. Sprinkle sesame seeds on top, then press it down.
3. Warm up your ninja Dual Zone Air Fryer to 180°C. Brush bread triangles using oil.
4. Put them in each cooking baskets, then cook within four mins per side till crispy. Serve.

Ingredients

300 grams prawns, peeled & cleaned - 50 grams water chestnuts, chopped - 15 grams spring onions, chopped - Two cloves garlic, minced - Five millilitres sesame oil - 10 millilitres soy sauce - 1 litre white bread loaf, sliced into triangles - 120 grams sesame seeds - 10 millilitres vegetable oil

NUTRITIONAL VALUES (PER SERVING): CALORIES: 420; CARBS: 38G; FAT: 20G; PROTEIN: 22G

Grilled Chicken
Caesar Wraps

🕐 **Prep:** *15 mins* 📦 **Cook:** *20 mins* 🍽 **Serves:** *4*

Directions

1. Warm up your ninja Dual Zone Air Fryer to 180°C. Flavour chicken breasts using salt plus pepper.
2. Put chicken breasts in each cooking basket, then cook within fifteen mins, flipping once. Cool it down, then slice into strips.
3. In your big container, mix lettuce, tomatoes, and dressing. Put sliced chicken among your four tortilla wraps.
4. Top each with salad mixture, plus Parmesan cheese. Fold in sides, then roll it up to seal. Serve.

Ingredients

500 grams no bones & skin chicken breasts - 200 grams romaine lettuce, chopped - 150 grams cherry tomatoes, halved - 100 grams Caesar salad dressing - 4 whole grain tortilla wraps - 30 grams Parmesan cheese, grated - Salt & pepper, as required

NUTRITIONAL VALUES (PER SERVING): CALORIES: 456; CARBS: 42G; FAT: 14G; PROTEIN: 35G

Air-Fried
Mini Quiches

 **Prep:** *15 mins*　 **Cook:** *12 mins*　🍽 **Serves:** *6*

Directions

1. In your big container, mix flour, salt plus butter till crumbly.
2. Add ice water slowly while mixing till a dough for. Flatten into a disc, wrap, then refrigerate within thirty mins.
3. Warm up your Ninja Dual Zone air fryer to 180°.
4. Roll out chilled dough to about three millimetres thick on your clean surface. Slice out twelve circles, then press them into your oiled mini-muffin tin.
5. In your separate container, mix cheese, bacon, eggs, milk, salt plus pepper. Spoon it into your pastry cases.
6. Place filled tins in your cooking basket, then cook within twelve mins till golden brown. Serve.

Ingredients

300 grams flour, all-purpose - 150 grams cold unsalted butter, cubed - 50 millilitres ice water Salt, as required - 100 grams cheddar cheese, grated - 200 grams cooked & crumbled bacon - Six big eggs, beaten - 60 millilitres milk - Salt & pepper, as required

NUTRITIONAL VALUES (PER SERVING): CALORIES: 335; CARBS: 27G; FAT: 20G; PROTEIN: 12G

Mediterranean
Vegetable Tartlets

 **Prep:** *15 mins*　 **Cook:** *20 mins*　🍽 **Serves:** *4*

Directions

1. Warm up your Ninja Dual Zone Air Fryer to 200°C.
2. Roll out puff pastry on your lightly floured surface till about three millimetres thick. Slice into four squares.
3. In your big container, mix cherry tomatoes, zucchini, bell pepper, onion, olive oil, garlic, salt, plus pepper.
4. Split mixture onto each puff pastry square. Fold edges of your pastry to create a small rim, then press gently to seal.
5. Put tartlets in your zone one cooking basket, then cook within eighteen to twenty mins till crispy. Serve.

Ingredients

200 grams puff pastry - 150 grams cherry tomatoes, halved - 100 grams zucchini, thinly sliced lengthwise - 100 grams yellow bell pepper, thinly sliced - 100 grams red onion, thinly sliced - Two cloves garlic, minced - 30 millilitres olive oil Five grams fresh basil leaves, chopped - Salt & pepper, as required

NUTRITIONAL VALUES (PER SERVING): CALORIES: 425; CARBS: 35G; FAT: 27G; PROTEIN: 6G

Crispy Tuna Melt Pockets

🕐 **Prep:** *15 mins*   📷 **Cook:** *10 mins*   🍽 **Serves:** *4*

Directions

1. In your container, mix tuna, cheddar cheese, mayonnaise, green onions, salt, plus pepper.
2. Lay four bread slices on your flat surface, then put tuna mixture onto each slice. Put remaining bread slices on top to close.
3. Spread some butter on all sides of each sandwich, then coat each using breadcrumbs.
4. Warm up your Ninja Dual Zone Air Fryer at 180°C. Put two sandwiches in each cooking basket, then cook within ten mins till crispy. Remove, cool it down, slice, then serve.

Ingredients

200 grams canned tuna, strained - 100 grams grated cheddar cheese - 50 grams mayonnaise = 30 grams sliced green onions - Two grams salt - One-gram black pepper, ground - Eight whole wheat bread slices - 50 grams softened butter - 100 grams breadcrumbs

NUTRITIONAL VALUES (PER SERVING): CALORIES: 435; CARBS: 38G; FAT: 21G; PROTEIN: 27G

Air-Fried Scotch Pies

🕐 **Prep:** *20 mins*   📷 **Cook:** *20 mins*   🍽 **Serves:** *4*

Directions

1. In your big container, mix flour, lard, water, plus salt till a dough forms. Form it into four circles. Line each pie tin using dough circles.
2. In your separate container, mix beef, salt, pepper, and Worcestershire. Put beef mixture among your pie tins. Crimp edges to seal your pies.
3. Warm up your ninja Dual Zone Air Fryer to 180°C. Put Scotch pies in zone one basket, then put potatoes in your zone two basket.
4. Cook within ten mins, switch basket and cook within ten mins till golden brown.
5. Meanwhile, boil broth in your small saucepan. Add potatoes, then simmer within fifteen mins till tender. Strain. Serve Scotch pies with potatoes.

Ingredients

500 grams minced beef - 200 grams plain flour - 100 grams lard - 100 millilitres water - Two grams salt - One-gram black pepper - 1.5 kilograms potatoes, peeled & chopped - 250 millilitres beef broth - 25 millilitres Worcestershire sauce

NUTRITIONAL VALUES (PER SERVING): CALORIES: 536; CARBS: 43G; FAT: 19G; PROTEIN: 28G

Cornish Pasty Bites

🕐 **Prep:** *20* mins   🍲 **Cook:** *15* mins   🍽 **Serves:** *4*

Directions

1. In your big container, mix the flour plus butter cubes till crumbly.
2. Slowly pour water, then mix till a firm dough form. Flatten into a disk, wrap, then refrigerate within thirty mins.
3. Mix vegetables, beef skirt, onion, salt, plus pepper in your big container. Warm up your ninja Dual Zone Air Fryer to 200°C.
4. Roll out chilled dough on your lightly floured surface. Slice into circles.
5. Put some filling on each dough circle. Fold it over your filling, then crimp edges to seal. Brush each pasty bite using egg wash.
6. Put them in each cooking basket zone, then cook within fifteen mins till golden brown.

Ingredients

500 grams flour, all-purpose - 250 grams cold unsalted butter, cubed - 100 millilitres ice-cold water - 1-kilogram mixed vegetables, chopped - 500 grams beef skirt, cubed - 100 grams onion, sliced - Salt & pepper, as required - One egg, beaten

NUTRITIONAL VALUES (PER SERVING): CALORIES: 800; CARBS: 82G; FAT: 35G; PROTEIN: 41G

Lamb Kofta Skewers

🕐 **Prep:** *20* mins   🍲 **Cook:** *10* mins   🍽 **Serves:** *4*

Directions

1. In your big container, mix lamb, bread crumbs, onion, garlic, oil, cumin, coriander, salt, plus black pepper. Add mint, then mix well.
2. Divide it into twelve, then shape each around your skewer. Warm up your ninja Dual Zone Air Fryer to 200°C.
3. Put skewers in each cooking basket zone, then cook within ten mins, turning once. Serve.

Ingredients

500 grams minced lamb - 100 grams bread crumbs - 70 grams onion, chopped - Six grams garlic, minced - 30 millilitres olive oil - 10 grams ground cumin - 10 grams ground coriander Five grams salt - Two grams black pepper - 30 millilitres fresh mint, chopped

NUTRITIONAL VALUES (PER SERVING): CALORIES: 475; CARBS: 13G; FAT: 33G; PROTEIN: 31G

Veggie
Burger Sliders

🕐 **Prep:** *15 mins*   📟 **Cook:** *15 mins*   🍽 **Serves:** *4*

Directions

1. In your big container, mix veggie burger mix, breadcrumbs, cheese, egg, salt, plus pepper. Form it into eight, then shape each into a small burger patty.
2. Warm up your Ninja Dual Zone Air Fryer to 190°C.
3. Brush each patty using oil, then put them in each cooking basket zone. Cook within fourteen mins, flipping once till golden.
4. Put cooked patty on each bottom half bun. Add ketchup, salad greens, then close using top half of your bun. Serve.

Ingredients

400 grams veggie burger mix - 100 grams breadcrumbs - 50 grams cheddar cheese, grated - One egg (beaten) - 30 millilitres olive oil - Eight slider buns, halved & toasted - 100 grams mixed salad greens - 50 millilitres ketchup - Salt & pepper, as required

NUTRITIONAL VALUES (PER SERVING): CALORIES: 450; CARBS: 55G; FAT: 18G; PROTEIN: 21G

Chilli & Lime
Halloumi Sticks

🕐 **Prep:** *10 mins*   📟 **Cook:** *10 mins*   🍽 **Serves:** *4*

Directions

1. In your small container, mix yogurt, chilli powder, paprika, zest, plus juice. Coat halloumi sticks using your marinade.
2. Warm up your Ninja Dual Zone Air Fryer to 190°C.
3. Put marinated halloumi sticks in each greased cooking basket zone. Cook within ten mins till crisp. Serve.

Ingredients

500 grams halloumi cheese, sliced into sticks
200 millilitres yogurt
Three grams chilli powder
Two grams paprika
Zest of one lime
30 millilitres lime juice
30 millilitres olive oil

NUTRITIONAL VALUES (PER SERVING): CALORIES: 455; CARBS: 9G; FAT: 37G; PROTEIN: 24G

BLT Sandwich
Toasties

🕐 **Prep:** *10 mins*   ▢ **Cook:** *8 mins*   🍽 **Serves:** *2*

Directions

1. Warm up your ninja Dual Zone Air Fryer at 180°C. Cook bacon in your cooking basket within four mins till crispy.
2. Put two bread slices on your working surface, then spread some mayonnaise on each.
3. Add lettuce, bacon, tomato, plus cheese on top. Close using rest bread slices.
4. Brush butter on each sandwich, put them in each cooking basket zone, then within four mins per side till golden brown. Serve.

Ingredients

Four bread slices
Six rashers of bacon
Two small tomatoes, sliced
50 grams shredded lettuce
100 grams cheddar cheese, grated
25 millilitres mayonnaise
25 millilitres unsalted butter, dissolved

NUTRITIONAL VALUES (PER SERVING): CALORIES: 650; CARBS: 40G; FAT: 42G; PROTEIN: 32G

Spiced
Samosa Pockets

🕐 **Prep:** *20 mins*   ▢ **Cook:** *10 mins*   🍽 **Serves:** *4*

Directions

1. In your pan with water, boil potatoes plus green peas till cooked.
2. Warm up oil in your separate pan, then cook onion till golden brown. Add ginger-garlic past, then cook within one min.
3. Mix in cooked potatoes & peas, garam masala powder, chili powder, coriander leaves, plus salt within three mins on low temp. Cool it down.
4. Warm up your ninja Dual Zone Air Fryer to 200°C.
5. Put some filling in each filo pastry square. Fold over, then seal edges using water.
6. Put samosa pockets into each cooking basket, then cook within ten mins till crispy, rotating once. Serve.

Ingredients

400 grams potatoes, peeled & diced - 100 grams green peas - 30 grams coriander leaves, chopped - 150 grams onion, chopped - 10 grams ginger-garlic paste - Five grams garam masala powder = Two grams chili powder - Salt, as required - 10 millilitres vegetable oil = Filo pastry sheets, sliced into 16 squares

NUTRITIONAL VALUES (PER SERVING): CALORIES: 320; CARBS: 47G; FAT: 11G; PROTEIN: 8G

Tomato & Basil
Bruschetta

🕐 **Prep:** *10 mins*   📲 **Cook:** *5 mins*   🍽 **Serves:** *4*

Directions

1. In your medium container, mix cherry tomatoes, oil, basil, plus garlic. Flavour it using salt plus pepper. Mix well, then put aside.
2. Warm up your ninja Dual Zone Air Fryer at 200°C.
3. Arrange ciabatta slices on your cooking trays, then cook them in your cooking basket within two to three mins till lightly toasted.
4. Remove your trays, then top each ciabatta slice using tomato mixture. Sprinkle Parmesan on top.
5. Put trays into your cooking basket, then cook within two mins. Serve.

Ingredients

300 grams cherry tomatoes, halved - 60 millilitres olive oil - 30 grams fresh basil, chopped - 1 garlic clove, minced - 100 grams Parmesan cheese, grated - 200 grams ciabatta bread, sliced - Salt & pepper, as required

NUTRITIONAL VALUES (PER SERVING): CALORIES: 497; CARBS: 42G; FAT: 28G; PROTEIN: 18G

Air-Fried
Falafel with Tahini Dip

🕐 **Prep:** *20 mins*   📲 **Cook:** *15 mins*   🍽 **Serves:** *4*

Directions

1. In your food processor, mix chickpeas, onion, parsley, cilantro, garlic, cumin, coriander, pepper flakes plus salt. Pulse till a coarse mixture form.
2. Transfer it to your big container, then mix flour. Let it rest within ten mins, then form it into patties.
3. Warm up your Ninja Dual Zone Air Fryer at 200°C. Put patties in each greased cooking basket zone.
4. Cook within fifteen mins, flipping once, till crispy.
5. Meanwhile, in your small container, whisk tahini paste, juice, garlic, and salt. Pour warm water while whisking till smooth. Serve it with falafel.

Ingredients

400 grams canned chickpeas, strained & washed - 100 grams onion, finely chopped - 15 grams fresh flat-leaf parsley, chopped - 15 grams fresh cilantro, chopped - Three garlic cloves, minced - Five grams ground cumin - Three grams ground coriander - One gram red pepper flakes - Two grams salt = 50 grams flour, all-purpose
For the Tahini Dip:
150 millilitres tahini paste- 30 millilitres lemon juice- Five grams garlic clove, minced - One gram salt - Quarter litre of warm water

NUTRITIONAL VALUES (PER SERVING): CALORIES: 350; CARBS: 40G; FAT: 16G; PROTEIN: 13G

Chicken
Tikka Wraps

🕐 **Prep:** *15 mins*　📱 **Cook:** *10 mins*　🍽 **Serves:** *4*

Directions

1. In your medium container, mix yogurt, juice, tikka spice mix, salt plus pepper. Add chicken strips, then mix well.
2. Warm up your Ninja Dual Zone Air Fryer to 190°C. Put chicken strips on one cooking basket. Cook within ten mins, flipping once. Remove, then cool it down.
3. Lay out each wrap on your plate, then put lettuce plus cucumber among them. Top each wrap using chicken tikka pieces plus coriander. Roll it up, then serve.

Ingredients

500 grams no bones & skin chicken breasts, sliced into thin strips - 200 grams Greek yogurt, plain - 50 millilitres lemon juice - 20 grams tikka spice mix - Four wholemeal wraps, warmed - Salt & pepper, as required
For serving:
200 grams shredded lettuce - 100 grams cucumber, thinly sliced

NUTRITIONAL VALUES (PER SERVING): CALORIES: 450; CARBS: 34G; FAT: 12G; PROTEIN: 45G

Garlic Mushroom
& Spinach Pies

🕐 **Prep:** *15 mins*　📱 **Cook:** *20 mins*　🍽 **Serves:** *4*

Directions

1. Warm up your ninja Dual Zone Air Fryer to 190°C.
2. In your big container, mix mushrooms, garlic, oil, salt, plus pepper.
3. Put spinach amongst each pastry square. Top with mushroom mixture.
4. Fold each pastry square to create a triangular pie shape, pressing edges to seal.
5. Place pies into each cooking basket zone. Cook within twenty mins till crispy. Serve.

Ingredients

400 grams puff pastry, sliced into four squares
300 grams chestnut mushrooms, sliced
100 grams baby spinach leaves
10 grams minced garlic
50 millilitres olive oil
Salt & pepper, as required

NUTRITIONAL VALUES (PER SERVING): CALORIES: 680; CARBS: 66G; FAT: 38G; PROTEIN: 12G

Vegetable
Tempura Selection

🕐 **Prep:** *15 mins*　　🍲 **Cook:** *10 mins*　　🍽 **Serves:** *4*

Directions

1. Warm up your ninja Dual Zone Air Fryer to 190°C.
2. In your medium container, whisk flour plus cornstarch. Pour ice-cold water, mixing till smooth.
3. Put mixed vegetables in your separate container, then flavour it using salt. Dip each vegetable into your batter.
4. Put them in each cooking basket zone. Cook within ten mins till crispy, turning once. Remove, cool it down, then serve.

Ingredients

100 grams mixed vegetables
50 grams plain flour
50 grams cornstarch
240 millilitres ice-cold water
Salt, as required

NUTRITIONAL VALUES (PER SERVING): CALORIES: 210; CARBS: 30G; FAT: 8G; PROTEIN: 4G

Welsh Cawl Soup
With Air-Fried Croutons

🕐 **Prep:** *15 mins*　　🍲 **Cook:** *1 h 30 mins*　　🍽 **Serves:** *6*

Directions

1. In your big pot on moderate temp, cook lamb within five mins, mixing often. Strain.
2. Add potatoes, parsnips, carrots, stock plus water. Let it boil, then simmer within one hour till vegetables are soft.
3. Warm up your Ninja Dual Zone air fryer to 180°C.
4. Put bread cubes in your zone one cooking basket. Lightly spray them using oil.
5. Cook croutons within four to six mins till crisp, shaking your basket once.
6. Mix in leeks in your soup, then cook within ten mins till soft. Flavour it using salt plus pepper. Serve hot with air-fried croutons.

Ingredients

400 grams lamb neck fillet, diced - One kg potatoes, peeled & diced - 500 grams parsnips, peeled & diced - 500 grams carrots, peeled & sliced - 750 millilitres chicken or vegetable stock - 250 millilitres water - 150 grams leeks, trimmed & thinly sliced - Salt & pepper, as required - 150 grams day-old bread, cubed

NUTRITIONAL VALUES (PER SERVING): CALORIES: 550; CARBS: 70G; FAT: 20G; PROTEIN: 35G

Beef
Wellington Bites

🕐 **Prep:** *20 mins*   📟 **Cook:** *15 mins*   🍽 **Serves:** *4*

Directions

1. Warm up your ninja Dual Zone Air Fryer to 200°C.
2. In your pan, dissolve butter, then cook mushrooms till softened. Add white wine, then cook till it thickens. Flavour it using salt plus pepper. Put aside.
3. Put beef tenderloin on each pastry square, then top using mushroom mixture. Fold corners, then press gently to seal.
4. Brush each bite using egg wash, then put them in each cooking basket. Cook within fifteen mins till crispy, turning once.

Ingredients

400 grams beef tenderloin, bite-sized cubes - 200 grams puff pastry, rolled out & sliced into squares - 100 grams mushrooms, chopped - 100 millilitres dry white wine - 50 grams unsalted butter - One big egg, beaten - Salt & pepper, as required

NUTRITIONAL VALUES (PER SERVING): CALORIES: 542; CARBS: 21G; FAT: 35G; PROTEIN: 37G

Air-Fried
Chicken Kiev

🕐 **Prep:** *20 mins*   📟 **Cook:** *25 mins*   🍽 **Serves:** *4*

Directions

1. In your small container, mix butter, garlic, juice, parsley, salt plus pepper. Put it in your fridge to chill within ten mins.
2. Slice a deep pocket into each chicken breast. Stuff each chicken pocket using chilled garlic butter, pressing edges to seal.
3. Put flour flavoured using salt plus pepper in one container, beaten eggs in second container, then put breadcrumbs on third.
4. Coat each chicken breast in flour, dip it in egg mixture, then coat it using breadcrumbs.
5. Warm up your Ninja Dual Zone Air Fryer to 180°C.
6. Put stuffed chicken breasts in each cooking basket zone, then cook within twenty-five mins till cooked. Serve.

Ingredients

Four no bones & skin chicken breasts - 200 grams breadcrumbs - 120 grams unsalted butter, softened - Four garlic cloves, minced - 50 millilitres lemon juice - 20 grams fresh parsley, finely chopped - 200 grams flour, all-purpose - 150 millilitres beaten eggs - Salt & pepper, as required

NUTRITIONAL VALUES (PER SERVING): CALORIES: 920; CARBS: 61G; FAT: 47G; PROTEIN: 69G

Classic Cottage
Pie Pots

⏱ **Prep:** *15 mins*   🍲 **Cook:** *45 mins*   🍽 **Serves:** *4*

Directions

1. Warm up your Ninja Dual Zone Air Fryer to 180°C.
2. In your big pan on moderate temp, cook minced beef within seven mins. Add onion, then cook within five mins.
3. Add carrots plus frozen peas, then cook within three mins.
4. Pour in broth, salt plus pepper, then simmer within fifteen mins on low temp.
5. Meanwhile, boil potatoes in your separate pot within ten mins till tender. Strain, then mash using milk plus butter till smooth. Flavour it using salt plus pepper.
6. Divide it among four ramekins, then top each with mashed potatoes.
7. Put filled pots in each cooking basket zone. Cook within twenty-five to thirty mins till golden brown.

Ingredients

500 grams lean minced beef - One-kilogram potatoes, peeled & chopped - 200 grams carrots, chopped - 100 grams frozen peas - One large onion, finely chopped - 500 millilitres beef broth - 200 millilitres milk - 50 grams butter - Salt & pepper, as required

NUTRITIONAL VALUES (PER SERVING): CALORIES: 520; CARBS: 46G; FAT: 20G; PROTEIN: 39G

Bangers & Mash
With Onion Gravy

⏱ **Prep:** *15 mins*   🍲 **Cook:** *25 mins*   🍽 **Serves:** *4*

Directions

1. Warm up your Ninja Dual Zone Air Fryer to 180°C.
2. Put sausages in one cooking basket zone, then cook within twenty-five mins, turning once.
3. Meanwhile, boil potatoes in your big pot with salted water within fifteen mins till tender. Strain, then mash with butter plus milk till smooth. Flavour it using salt plus pepper.
4. In your separate saucepan, dissolve some butter on moderate temp, then cook onions till soft. Mix in flour, then cook within two mins.
5. Slowly add stock, mixing till smooth. Serve mashed potatoes with two sausages plus some onion gravy.

Ingredients

Eight sausages - One kilogram potatoes, peeled & cubed - 50 grams butter - 100 millilitres milk - Salt & pepper, as required - 200 grams onions, thinly sliced - 30 grams plain flour - 500 millilitres beef stock

NUTRITIONAL VALUES (PER SERVING): CALORIES: 680; CARBS: 51G; FAT: 42G; PROTEIN: 27G

Salmon & Dill
Encrusted Parcels

🕐 **Prep:** *15 mins* 📠 **Cook:** *12 mins* 🍽 **Serves:** *4*

Directions

1. Warm up your ninja Dual Zone Air Fryer to 200°C.
2. In your small container, mix cream cheese, juice, and dill. Flavour it using salt plus pepper, mix well, then put aside.
3. Put each salmon fillet in puff pastry square. Spread some cream cheese mixture on top. Fold puff pastry, sealing edges to form parcels, then brush it using oil on top.
4. Put parcels in each cooking basket, then cook within twelve mins till puffed up. Serve.

Ingredients

Four (800 grams) fresh salmon fillets - 180 grams puff pastry, sliced into four squares - 100 grams cream cheese - 30 millilitres lemon juice - 20 grams fresh dill, chopped - Salt & pepper, as required - 10 millilitres olive oil

NUTRITIONAL VALUES (PER SERVING): CALORIES: 690; CARBS: 28G; FAT: 45G; PROTEIN: 42G

Vegan
Shepherd's Pie

🕐 **Prep:** *15 mins* 📠 **Cook:** *30 mins* 🍽 **Serves:** *4*

Directions

1. Warm up your ninja Dual Zone Air Fryer to 180°C.
2. Cook onions and garlic in your saucepan on moderate temp till softened.
3. Add vegetable mix, lentils, plus broth. Flavour it using salt plus pepper. Simmer within ten mins till vegetables are tender.
4. Meanwhile, boil potatoes in your separate pot till soft. Strain. Mash potatoes with milk plus vegan butter till smooth. Flavour it using salt plus pepper.
5. Transfer lentil-vegetable mixture into your air fryer-safe pan. Spread mashed potatoes on top.
6. Cook within thirty mins till golden brown. Serve.

Ingredients

300 grams lentils, cooked - 200 grams frozen vegetable mix - 100 grams onion, diced - Two cloves of garlic, minced - 500 millilitres vegetable broth - One kilogram potatoes, peeled & chopped - 200 millilitres non-dairy milk - 50 grams vegan butter - Salt & pepper, as required

NUTRITIONAL VALUES (PER SERVING): CALORIES: 490; CARBS: 75G; FAT: 15G; PROTEIN: 25G

Crispy Duck
With Plum Sauce

🕐 **Prep:** *20 mins*   ▣ **Cook:** *35 mins*   🍽 **Serves:** *4*

Directions

1. Warm up your ninja Dual Zone Air Fryer to 180°C.
2. Rub duck using sea salt plus Szechuan peppercorns. Put seasoned duck in your cooking basket zone one, then cook within twenty-five mins.
3. Meanwhile, mix plums, water, sugar, vinegar, plus ginger in your saucepan. Cook on moderate temp till it thickens.
4. Adjust air fryer to 200°C, then cook within ten mins till crispy. Remove the duck, then cool it down. Serve crispy duck with plum sauce.

Ingredients

One whole duck (1.5-2 kilograms), removed excess & pat dried - Three grams sea salt - Five grams Szechuan peppercorns, crushed - 300 grams plums, pitted & chopped - 50 millilitres water - 100 grams sugar - 25 millilitres red wine vinegar - 10 grams ginger, finely grated

NUTRITIONAL VALUES (PER SERVING): CALORIES: 573; CARBS: 32G; FAT: 38G; PROTEIN: 26G

Beef & Ale
Pie Pastries

🕐 **Prep:** *30 mins*   ▣ **Cook:** *25 mins*   🍽 **Serves:** *4*

Directions

1. In your big container, marinate beef in the ale within two hours.
2. Warm up your ninja Dual Zone air fryer to 180°C. Warm up oil in your big pan on moderate temp, then cook onions till translucent.
3. Remove marinated beef, reserving liquid, then put it to your pan with onions. Cook till browned.
4. Mix in flour, then cook within one min. Slowly pour in reserved ale marinade plus stock, mixing well.
5. Add mushrooms, salt, plus pepper, then let it simmer within ten mins till slightly thickened.
6. Roll out shortcrust pastry on your lightly floured surface, then slice into four squares.
7. Put beef mixture among each pastry square, fold them over, then seal edges.
8. Put filled pastries in your cooking basket one zone, then cook within twenty mins till golden brown. Serve.

Ingredients

500 grams diced beef - One litre ale - 200 grams onion, chopped - 150 grams mushrooms, sliced - 300 grams shortcrust pastry - 100 millilitres beef stock - 50 grams flour, all-purpose - 30 millilitres vegetable oil - Salt & pepper, as required

NUTRITIONAL VALUES (PER SERVING): CALORIES: 699; CARBS: 53G; FAT: 36G; PROTEIN: 35G

UK Stuffed
Bell Peppers

🕐 **Prep:** *20 mins*   📱 **Cook:** *12 mins*   🍽 **Serves:** *4*

Directions

1. Warm up your ninja Dual Zone Air Fryer to 190°C. Brush bell peppers using oil.
2. In your big container, mix mushrooms, tomatoes, onion, garlic, cooked quinoa, plus half of tomato sauce. Flavour it using salt plus pepper.
3. Put filling mixture in each bell pepper. Put stuffed bell peppers in your cooking basket one zone.
4. Cook within eight mins, pour rest of tomato sauce, then top using cheddar cheese. Cook within four mins till cheese is melted. Serve.

Ingredients

4 large bell peppers, sliced tops & seeded - 200 grams mushrooms, diced - 150 grams cherry tomatoes, quartered - 150 grams onion, chopped - Two cloves garlic, minced - 100 grams cooked quinoa or rice - 500 millilitres tomato sauce - 100 grams grated cheddar cheese - Olive oil for brushing

NUTRITIONAL VALUES (PER SERVING): CALORIES: 350; CARBS: 42G; FAT: 13G; PROTEIN: 17G

Pork Loin
With Apple Glaze

🕐 **Prep:** *10 mins*   📱 **Cook:** *25 mins*   🍽 **Serves:** *4*

Directions

1. Warm up your ninja Dual Zone air fryer to 200°C.
2. In your small container, mix honey, mustard, cinnamon, salt, plus pepper. Rub pork loin using oil, then flavour it using salt plus pepper.
3. Put pork loin in your cooking basket zone one. Cook within twenty mins.
4. Meanwhile, mix apples in half of your glaze mixture.
5. Ahe apple slices to your other cooking basket zone, then cook alongside your pork within five mins.
6. Remove pork, cool it down, slice, then glaze each pork slice using rest of glaze mixture. Serve it with cooked apples.

Ingredients

800 grams pork loin - 200 grams sliced apples - 30 millilitres honey - 30 millilitres mustard, whole grain - One gram ground cinnamon - Salt & pepper, as required - 15 millilitres vegetable oil

NUTRITIONAL VALUES (PER SERVING): CALORIES: 392; CARBS: 19G; FAT: 15G; PROTEIN: 47G

Grilled Sea Bass
With Lemon Butter

 **Prep:** *15 mins*    **Cook:** *12 mins*   **Serves:** *4*

Directions

1. In your small container, mix juice, zest, butter, garlic, plus oil. Flavour sea bass fillets using salt plus pepper.
2. Warm up your ninja Dual Zone Air Fryer to 200°C. Brush fillets using lemon butter mixture.
3. Put fillets into your cooking basket, then cook within six mins. Flip fillets, then brush them using rest of lemon butter mixture.
4. Cook within six mins till sea bass is cooked. Remove fillets, then pour any leftover lemon butter sauce on top.

Ingredients

Four sea bass fillets (200 grams each)
One lemon, juice & zest
100 grams unsalted butter, dissolved
Three garlic cloves, minced
60 millilitres olive oil
Salt & pepper, as required

NUTRITIONAL VALUES (PER SERVING): CALORIES: 430; CARBS: 2G; FAT: 31G; PROTEIN: 34G

Tikka Masala
Chicken Wings

 **Prep:** *15 mins*    **Cook:** *20 mins*   **Serves:** *4*

Directions

1. In your big container, mix yogurt, tikka masala, juice, garlic, ginger, paprika, cumin, salt plus pepper.
2. Add chicken wings, then mix well. Marinate within two hours in your refrigerator. Warm up your Ninja Dual Zone air fryer to 180°C.
3. Put your chicken wings into your cooking basket zone one. Cook within twenty mins, flipping once. Remove, cool it down, then serve.

Ingredients

One kilogram chicken wings - 200 grams plain Greek yogurt - 100 millilitres tikka masala sauce - 30 millilitres lemon juice - Two grams grated garlic - Two grams grated ginger - Five grams ground paprika - Five grams ground cumin - Salt & pepper, as required

NUTRITIONAL VALUES (PER SERVING): CALORIES: 465; CARBS: 10G; FAT: 27G; PROTEIN: 39G

Rosemary
Lamb Chops

🕐 Prep: *10* mins 　 📲 Cook: *12* mins 　 🍽 Serves: *4*

Directions

1. In your big container, mix oil, rosemary, garlic, salt, plus pepper. Add lamb chops, mixing well. Marinate within ten mins.
2. Warm up your Ninja Dual Zone Air Fryer to 200°C.
3. Split lamb chops in each cooking basket zone, then cook within six mins per side. Remove, cool it down, then serve.

Ingredients

Eight (800 grams) lamb chops, bone-in
30 millilitres olive oil
10 grams fresh rosemary, chopped
Four grams garlic cloves, minced
Salt & pepper, as required

NUTRITIONAL VALUES (PER SERVING): CALORIES: 400; CARBS: 1G; FAT: 32G; PROTEIN: 27G

Vegetarian
Lasagne Cups

🕐 Prep: *15* mins 　 📲 Cook: *25* mins 　 🍽 Serves: *4*

Directions

1. Warm up your Ninja Dual Zone air fryer to 180°C.
2. Cook lasagne sheets in broth till tender. Strain, then put aside.
3. In your container, mix ricotta cheese, spinach, Parmesan, salt, plus pepper.
4. Split half cooked lasagne sheets among four ramekins.
5. Spread some ricotta mixture on each, add some tomato sauce, then sprinkle using mozzarella plus cheddar cheese.
6. Put another lasagne sheets layer, ricotta mixture, tomato sauce, plus both mozzarella & cheddar cheese.
7. Put ramekins into each cooking basket zone. Cook within twenty-five mins till golden brown. Remove, cool it down, then serve.

Ingredients

200 grams lasagne sheets, broken into pieces - 500 grams tomato sauce - 200 grams ricotta cheese - 100 grams grated mozzarella cheese - 100 grams grated cheddar cheese - 100 grams chopped spinach (frozen, thawed) - 50 grams grated Parmesan cheese - 500 millilitres vegetable broth - Salt & pepper, as required

NUTRITIONAL VALUES (PER SERVING): CALORIES: 467; CARBS: 49G; FAT: 23G; PROTEIN: 21G

Creamy Chicken
& Leek Pie

🕐 **Prep:** *15 mins*   📟 **Cook:** *40 mins*   🍽 **Serves:** *4*

Directions

1. Warm up your Ninja Dual Zone Air Fryer to 180°C.
2. In your big pan, dissolve butter on moderate temp. Add leeks, then cook within five mins till softened.
3. Add chicken, then cook within five mins till browned. Mix in flour, then cook within two mins. Add stock while mixing within two mins.
4. Mix in double cream, then flavour it using salt plus pepper. Put aside.
5. Split cooled chicken-leek mixture among your four pastry rectangles. Fold over, then crimp edges to seal.
6. Transfer pies onto each lined cooking basket within twenty mins, swapping basket once till brown. Serve.

Ingredients

400 grams no bones & skin chicken breast, diced - 300 grams leeks, washed and sliced - 50 grams butter - 50 grams plain flour - 300 millilitres chicken stock - 150 millilitres double cream - Salt & pepper, as required - 500 grams puff pastry, ready-made, rolled out & sliced into four rectangles

NUTRITIONAL VALUES (PER SERVING): CALORIES: 674; CARBS: 60G; FAT: 37G; PROTEIN: 32G

Traditional
Lancashire Hotpot

🕐 **Prep:** *20 mins*   📟 **Cook:** *1 h 30 mins*   🍽 **Serves:** *4-5*

Directions

1. In your container, marinate lamb using Worcestershire, salt, plus pepper within ten mins.
2. Warm up your ninja Dual Zone Air Fryer to 180°C. Put half potatoes in your cooking basket, then put marinated lamb on top.
3. Add onions, carrots, mushrooms plus stock. Put rest of potatoes, then brush it using butter.
4. Cook within one hour and thirty mins till cooked. Serve.

Ingredients

800 grams lamb shoulder, diced - 600 grams potatoes, thinly sliced - 300 grams onions, chopped - 150 grams carrots, chopped - 100 grams mushrooms, sliced - 2 litres beef stock - 20 grams Worcestershire sauce - Salt & pepper, as required

NUTRITIONAL VALUES (PER SERVING): CALORIES: 624; CARBS: 32G; FAT: 35G; PROTEIN: 44G

Seared Teriyaki
Tuna Steaks

🕐 **Prep:** *15* mins   🍲 **Cook:** *8* mins   🍽 **Serves:** *4*

Directions

1. In your shallow container, mix teriyaki sauce plus oil. Add tuna steaks, then marinate within ten mins.
2. Warm up your Ninja Dual Zone Air Fryer to 200°C.
3. Take marinated tuna steaks, then flavour it using salt plus black pepper. Put tuna steaks in your cooking basket zone one.
4. Cook within four mins per side till cooked. Sprinkle sesame seeds, then serve each seared teriyaki tuna steak over mixed salad greens.

Ingredients

Four tuna steaks (150 grams each) - 60 millilitres teriyaki sauce - 30 millilitres olive oil - 20 grams sesame seeds - Two grams salt - One gram ground black pepper - Two kilograms mixed salad greens

NUTRITIONAL VALUES (PER SERVING): CALORIES: 370; CARBS: 6G; FAT: 14G; PROTEIN: 50G

Ratatouille
Stuffed Aubergines

🕐 **Prep:** *25* mins   🍲 **Cook:** *20* mins   🍽 **Serves:** *4*

Directions

1. Warm up your Ninja Dual Zone Air Fryer to 180°C.
2. Chop up aubergine flesh, then mix it with the tomatoes, bell peppers, courgettes, onion, plus garlic.
3. Put mixed vegetables in one cooking basket, then drizzle them using oil. Flavour it using salt plus pepper.
4. Cook within ten mins, mixing once. Cook again within ten mins till vegetables are soft. Remove them.
5. Put cooked ratatouille mixture in each hollowed-out aubergine. Cook again within five to seven mins till warmed. Serve.

Ingredients

Two big aubergines, sliced half lengthwise & scooped out flesh - 200 grams cherry tomatoes, halved - 100 grams bell peppers, chopped - 100 grams courgettes, chopped - 150 grams onion, chopped - Five grams garlic, minced - 30 millilitres olive oil - Salt & pepper, as required

NUTRITIONAL VALUES (PER SERVING): CALORIES: 190; CARBS: 27G; FAT: 8G; PROTEIN: 4G

Spaghetti
Carbonara Bowls

🕐 **Prep:** *15* mins   🍲 **Cook:** *20* mins   🍽 **Serves:** *4*

Directions

1. In your container, whisk eggs, heavy cream, plus Parmesan. Flavour it using salt plus pepper. Put aside. Warm up your ninja Dual Zone air fryer to 180°C.
2. In your medium container, mix pancetta plus oil. Put pancetta on your cooking basket zone one. Cook within ten mins till crispy, mixing once.
3. In your large skillet on low temp, add cooked spaghetti plus pancetta. Slowly add egg mixture while mixing.
4. Cook within five mins till sauce has thickened. Serve.

Ingredients

400 grams uncooked spaghetti, cooked
150 grams pancetta, diced
Three big eggs
100 millilitres heavy cream
50 grams Parmesan cheese, grated
Salt & pepper, as required
15 millilitres olive oil

NUTRITIONAL VALUES (PER SERVING): CALORIES: 635; CARBS: 66G; FAT: 31G; PROTEIN: 26G

Air-Fried
Steak & Ale Puddings

🕐 **Prep:** *30* mins   🍲 **Cook:** *20* mins   🍽 **Serves:** *4*

Directions

1. In your container, marinate steak in dark ale within one hour. Warm up your Ninja Dual Zone air fryer to 200°C.
2. In your big saucepan, warm up oil on moderate temp, then onion plus carrots till softened.
3. Mix in marinated steak, then cook within five mins. Mix in flour, then cook within two mins. Add stock, salt plus pepper. Simmer within ten mins.
4. Split puff pastry into four, then roll out each into a thin sheet.
5. Fill each pudding container using steak mixture, then cover using pastry sheet, pressing edges to seal.
6. Put prepared pudding containers into your cooking basket zone one, then cook within twenty mins till golden brown.
7. Meanwhile, boil your potatoes till tender, then mash them using some butter plus warm milk till smooth. Serve each pudding with mashed potatoes plus peas.

Ingredients

500 grams beef steak, diced - 300 millilitres dark ale - One kilogram potatoes, peeled & chopped - 100 grams frozen peas, steamed - 200 grams puff pastry - One onion, chopped - Two carrots, chopped - 30 millilitres vegetable oil - 50 grams flour, all-purpose - 240 millilitres beef stock - Salt & pepper, as required

NUTRITIONAL VALUES (PER SERVING): CALORIES: 865; CARBS: 62G; FAT: 40G; PROTEIN: 52G

Honey-Glazed
Parsnip Sticks

🕐 **Prep:** *10 mins*   ▦ **Cook:** *15 mins*   🍽 **Serves:** *4*

Directions

1. Warm up your ninja Dual Zone Air Fryer to 200°C.
2. In your container, mix parsnip, oil, salt, plus pepper. Split parsnip sticks in each cooking basket, then cook within ten mins.
3. Meanwhile, in your small saucepan on low temp, warm up honey, then mix in cinnamon till blended.
4. Remove cooked parsnip sticks, then move them to your container with honey-cinnamon mixture. Mix well.
5. Put glazed parsnip sticks to each cooking basket, then cook within five mins till crispy.

Ingredients

600 grams parsnips, peeled & sliced into sticks
15 millilitres vegetable oil
100 grams honey
Two grams cinnamon, ground
Salt & pepper, as required

NUTRITIONAL VALUES (PER SERVING): CALORIES: 275; CARBS: 45G; FAT: 11G; PROTEIN: 3G

Red Cabbage
& Apple Slaw

🕐 **Prep:** *15 mins*   ▦ **Cook:** *10 mins*   🍽 **Serves:** *4*

Directions

1. Warm up your Ninja Dual Zone Air Fryer to 180°C.
2. In your big container, mix cabbage, apples, carrot, plus onion.
3. In your small container, whisk mayonnaise, apple cider, plus mustard till smooth.
4. Add it on slaw mixture, then toss well. Flavour it using salt plus pepper. Put slaw in each cooking basket, then cook within ten mins, tossing once. Serve.

Ingredients

300 grams red cabbage, thinly sliced - 200 grams apples, thinly sliced - 150 grams carrot, grated - 50 grams red onion, thinly sliced - 100 millilitres mayonnaise - 50 millilitres apple cider vinegar - 10 grams Dijon mustard - Salt & pepper, as required

NUTRITIONAL VALUES (PER SERVING): CALORIES: 210; CARBS: 18G; FAT: 14G; PROTEIN: 2G

Crispy Cauliflower Bites
With Yogurt Dip

🕐 **Prep:** *15* mins   🍲 **Cook:** *20* mins   🍽 **Serves:** *4*

Directions

1. Warm up your Ninja Dual Zone Air Fryer to 190°C.
2. In your big container, whisk flour, powdered garlic, paprika, salt, plus pepper. Slowly pour milk while mixing till smooth.
3. In another container, add panko breadcrumbs. Dip each cauliflower floret in batter, then coat in breadcrumbs.
4. Put breaded cauliflower bites into your cooking basket, then cook within twenty mins till crispy, turning once.
5. In your small container, mix yogurt, juice, plus chives. Flavour it using salt plus pepper. Serve cauliflower bites with yogurt dip.

Ingredients

600 grams cauliflower florets - 120 grams flour, all-purpose - Two grams powdered garlic - Two grams paprika - Two grams salt - One gram black pepper - 200 millilitres milk - 100 grams panko breadcrumbs
For the Yogurt Dip:
250 millilitres plain yogurt - 20 millilitres lemon juice - 10 grams chopped fresh chives - Salt & pepper, as required

NUTRITIONAL VALUES (PER SERVING): CALORIES: 303; CARBS: 43G; FAT: 6G; PROTEIN: 14G

Zucchini
& Parmesan Rounds

🕐 **Prep:** *15* mins   🍲 **Cook:** *10* mins   🍽 **Serves:** *4*

Directions

1. Warm up your ninja Dual Zone Air Fryer to 200°C.
2. In your big container, mix zucchini slices, oil, salt, plus pepper.
3. In your separate shallow container, mix Parmesan plus breadcrumbs.
4. Dip each zucchini into Parmesan-breadcrumb mixture, pressing gently.
5. Put coated zucchini in each greased cooking basket zone. Cook within ten mins till crispy. Serve.

Ingredients

600 grams zucchini, sliced into 1cm rounds
150 grams Parmesan cheese, grated
120 millilitres olive oil
80 grams breadcrumbs
Two grams each salt & ground black pepper

NUTRITIONAL VALUES (PER SERVING): CALORIES: 410; CARBS: 21G; FAT: 31G; PROTEIN: 15G

Mini
Yorkshire Puddings

🕐 **Prep:** *15 mins*　　📦 **Cook:** *15 mins*　　🍽 **Serves:** *6*

Directions

1. In your big container, whisk flour, eggs, milk, plus salt till smooth. Let it rest within ten mins.
2. Warm up your ninja Dual Zone Air Fryer to 220°C. Brush oil among each six-hole silicone muffin tin. Put in your cooking basket to warm up.
3. Pour batter into each muffin tin, move them in your cooking basket zone one, then cook within fifteen mins till golden. Serve.

Ingredients

100 grams plain flour
Two big eggs
300 millilitres milk
Salt, as required
30 millilitres vegetable oil

NUTRITIONAL VALUES (PER SERVING): CALORIES: 148; CARBS: 16G; FAT: 6G; PROTEIN: 7G

Pesto & Pine Nut
Stuffed Mushrooms

🕐 **Prep:** *15 mins*　　📦 **Cook:** *12 mins*　　🍽 **Serves:** *4*

Directions

1. Warm up your ninja Dual Zone Air Fryer to 180°C.
2. In your container, mix cream cheese, pesto, pine nuts, Parmesan, salt, plus pepper. Stuff each mushroom with it.
3. Put stuffed mushrooms in each cooking basket zone, then cook within twelve mins till golden. Serve.

Ingredients

Sixteen big Portobello mushrooms, cleaned
& stalks removed - 200 grams cream cheese,
softened - 100 grams pesto - 100 grams pine nuts,
toasted - 50 grams Parmesan cheese, grated -
Salt & pepper, as required - 10 millilitres olive oil

NUTRITIONAL VALUES (PER SERVING): CALORIES: 450; CARBS: 14G; FAT: 38G; PROTEIN: 17G

Cheesy Leek
& Potato Bites

🕐 **Prep:** *15 mins*   🍲 **Cook:** *20 mins*   🍽 **Serves:** *4*

Directions

1. Warm up your ninja Dual Zone air fryer to 200°C.
2. In your big container, mix potatoes, two-thirds of oil, salt plus pepper.
3. Put seasoned potatoes in your cooking basket zone one, then cook within ten mins.
4. Meanwhile, warm up rest of oil in your pan on moderate temp, then cook leeks within five mins till softened.
5. In your separate container, mix cooked leeks, cheddar plus double cream.
6. Add leek-cheese mixture on potatoes, then cook within ten mins till cheese is melted. Serve.

Ingredients

400 grams potatoes, peeled & diced
300 grams leeks, thinly sliced
150 grams cheddar cheese, grated
100 millilitres double cream
60 millilitres vegetable oil
Salt & pepper, as required

NUTRITIONAL VALUES (PER SERVING): CALORIES: 521; CARBS: 34G; FAT: 37G; PROTEIN: 14G

Spiced Sweet
Potato Wedges

🕐 **Prep:** *10 mins*   🍲 **Cook:** *20 mins*   🍽 **Serves:** *4*

Directions

1. Warm up your Ninja Dual Zone air fryer at 200°C.
2. In your big container, mix sweet potatoes, oil, cumin, paprika, cinnamon, salt, plus pepper.
3. Arrange sweet potato wedges in each cooking basket zone. Cook within ten mins, switch basket, then cook within ten mins till crispy. Serve.

Ingredients

600 grams sweet potatoes, washed, pat dried, & sliced into wedges - 30 millilitres olive oil - Five grams cumin, ground - Five grams paprika, smoked - Two grams cinnamon, ground - Salt & pepper, as required

NUTRITIONAL VALUES (PER SERVING): CALORIES: 220; CARBS: 28G; FAT: 10G; PROTEIN: 3G

Green Bean
& Almond Toss

🕐 **Prep:** *10* mins   🍲 **Cook:** *8* mins   🛎 **Serves:** *4*

Directions

1. Warm up your ninja Dual Zone air fryer to 200°C.
2. In your container, mix green beans, almonds, plus oil. Flavour it using salt plus pepper.
3. Split green bean-almond mixture into your two baskets, then cook within eight mins, shaking your baskets once. Remove, then cool it down. Drizzle lemon juice on top. Serve.

Ingredients

500 grams green beans, trimmed
50 grams almonds, roughly chopped
15 millilitres olive oil
Salt & pepper, as required
10 millilitres lemon juice

NUTRITIONAL VALUES (PER SERVING): CALORIES: 168; CARBS: 12G; FAT: 11G; PROTEIN: 6G

Scotch Bonnet
Chicken Wings

🕐 **Prep:** *15* mins   🍲 **Cook:** *25* mins   🛎 **Serves:** *4*

Directions

1. In your big container, mix bonnet pepper, garlic, ginger, soy sauce, honey, plus lime juice.
2. Add chicken wings, then toss till coated. Marinate within one hour in your fridge. Warm up your Ninja Dual Zone Air Fryer to 200°C.
3. Take marinated chicken wings, then flavour it using salt plus pepper.
4. Put chicken wings in each cooking basket zone, then cook within twenty-five mins, flipping once. Serve.

Ingredients

One kilogram chicken wings - 30 grams Scotch bonnet pepper, chopped - Five grams garlic, minced - 20 grams ginger, grated - 100 millilitres soy sauce - 50 millilitres honey - 15 millilitres lime juice - Salt & pepper, as required

NUTRITIONAL VALUES (PER SERVING): CALORIES: 450; CARBS: 17G; FAT: 27G; PROTEIN: 35G

Olive & Cheese
Stuffed Bread Balls

🕐 **Prep:** *15 mins*   🍲 **Cook:** *12 mins*   🍽 **Serves:** *4*

Directions

1. In your big container, mix flour, yeast, sugar, plus salt. Slowly add warm water, then mix till a dough form.
2. Knead it on your floured surface within five mins till elastic. Put dough in your oiled container, cover, then let it rest within one hour till doubled in size.
3. Warm up your ninja Dual Zone air fryer to 180°C.
4. Divide dough into twelve, then flatten each. Fill it with olives plus cheese. Fold sides to cover filling, then shape it into ball.
5. Put stuffed bread balls into each cooking basket zone, then cook within twelve mins till golden brown. Serve.

Ingredients

250 grams flour, all-purpose - 1.5 grams instant yeast - Five grams sugar - Three grams salt - 125 millilitres warm water - 30 millilitres olive oil - 100 grams pitted black olives, chopped - 100 grams cheddar cheese, cubes

NUTRITIONAL VALUES (PER SERVING): CALORIES: 450; CARBS: 46G; FAT: 21G; PROTEIN: 18G

Crispy Kale Chips
With Sea Salt

🕐 **Prep:** *10 mins*   🍲 **Cook:** *10 mins*   🍽 **Serves:** *4*

Directions

1. Warm up your ninja Dual Zone Air Fryer to 200°C.
2. In your big container, mix kale plus oil. Put oiled kale in each cooking basket zone.
3. Cook within five mins, switch basket, then cook within five mins till crispy. Serve.

Ingredients

200 grams kale, washed, dried, stems removed & tore - 15 millilitres olive oil - Five grams sea salt

NUTRITIONAL VALUES (PER SERVING): CALORIES: 72; CARBS: 6G; FAT: 4G; PROTEIN: 3G

Roasted Beetroot & Feta Salad

🕐 **Prep:** *15 mins*　　🍲 **Cook:** *35 mins*　　🍽 **Serves:** *4*

Directions

1. Warm up your ninja Dual Zone Air Fryer to 180°C.
2. In your big container, mix beetroot, 50 millilitres oil, salt, plus black pepper.
3. Put beetroot in your cooking basket zone one, then cook within thirty-five mins, shaking once till beetroot is tender.
4. In your small container, mix rest of oil, honey, plus vinegar till smooth.
5. In your salad container, mix greens plus cooked beetroot. Add dressing, then mix well. Top it using feta cheese, then serve.

Ingredients

600 grams beetroot, peeled & diced - 200 grams feta cheese, crumbled - 100 millilitres olive oil - 30 grams honey - 50 millilitres balsamic vinegar - Three grams salt - Two grams black pepper, ground - One kilogram mixed greens

NUTRITIONAL VALUES (PER SERVING): CALORIES: 410; CARBS: 32G; FAT: 27G; PROTEIN: 9G

Mini Corn-on-the-Cob With Herb Butter

🕐 **Prep:** *10 mins*　　🍲 **Cook:** *12 mins*　　🍽 **Serves:** *4*

Directions

1. In your small container, mix butter, juice, parsley, chives, salt, plus pepper. Put aside. Warm up your Ninja Dual Zone Air Fryer to 200°C.
2. Spread herb butter on each corn, put them in your cooking basket zone one. Cook within twelve mins till slightly golden. Serve.

Ingredients

Eight mini corn-on-the-cob, washed & pat dried - 100 grams unsalted butter, softened - 15 millilitres lemon juice - 30 grams parsley, chopped - 30 grams chives, chopped - Salt & pepper, as required

NUTRITIONAL VALUES (PER SERVING): CALORIES: 320; CARBS: 24G; FAT: 24G; PROTEIN: 5G

Garlic & Herb
Potato Croquettes

🕐 **Prep:** *15* mins   🍲 **Cook:** *20* mins   🍽 **Serves:** *4*

Directions

1. In your big container, mash cooked potatoes with garlic, Parmesan cheese, salt, plus pepper. Shape it into small croquette shapes.
2. Put bread crumbs onto your flat plate, then roll each croquette in it. Warm up your ninja Dual Zone Air Fryer to 200°C.
3. Split croquettes into each cooking basket zone, then cook within twenty mins till golden brown, turning once. Serve.

Ingredients

800 grams potatoes, peeled, cubed & boiled - 100 grams bread crumbs - 50 grams grated Parmesan cheese - Two cloves garlic, minced - 10 millilitres olive oil - Salt & pepper, as required

NUTRITIONAL VALUES (PER SERVING): CALORIES: 350; CARBS: 48G; FAT: 12G; PROTEIN: 12G

Caramelised Onion & Goat's
Cheese Tartlets

🕐 **Prep:** *15* mins   🍲 **Cook:** *20* mins   🍽 **Serves:** *6*

Directions

1. Warm up your ninja Dual Zone air fryer to 180°C.
2. In your pan, warm up oil on moderate temp, add onions, then cook them within five to seven mins till golden brown.
3. Add vinegar, salt, plus black pepper, then cook within three mins. Put each pastry square in each cooking basket zone.
4. Split caramelised onions among your pastry squares. Put crumbled goat's cheese on top, then sprinkle using thyme.
5. Cook within fifteen to twenty mins till golden brown. Remove, cool it down, then serve.

Ingredients

300 grams puff pastry, rolled out & sliced into six squares - 200 grams goat's cheese - 300 grams onions, thinly sliced - 30 millilitres olive oil - 15 millilitres balsamic vinegar - Five grams thyme, chopped - Five grams salt - Two grams black pepper

NUTRITIONAL VALUES (PER SERVING): CALORIES: 350; CARBS: 33G; FAT: 20G; PROTEIN: 10G

Piri Piri Prawn Skewers

🕐 **Prep:** *15 mins*　📠 **Cook:** *10 mins*　🔔 **Serves:** *4*

Directions

1. In your container, mix prawns plus 50 millilitres piri piri sauce. Marinate within ten mins.
2. Warm up your Ninja Dual Zone Air Fryer to 200°C.
3. Thread marinated prawns, bell pepper plus onion onto skewers.
4. In another small container, mix rest of piri piri sauce plus oil. Brush this mixture onto your skewers, then flavour it using salt plus black pepper.
5. Put skewers in each cooking basket zone, then cook within ten mins till prawns are cooked through, turning once.

Ingredients

600 grams raw king prawns, peeled & cleaned
200 grams red bell peppers, sliced into 2cm pieces
150 grams red onion wedges
100 millilitres piri piri sauce (store-bought)
30 millilitres olive oil
Salt & black pepper, as required

NUTRITIONAL VALUES (PER SERVING): CALORIES: 348; CARBS: 13G; FAT: 14G; PROTEIN: 41G

Beetroot Hummus & Pita Triangles

🕐 **Prep:** *15 mins*　📠 **Cook:** *10 mins*　🔔 **Serves:** *4*

Directions

1. In your food processor, mix chickpeas, beetroot, garlic, tahini, juice plus thirty millilitres oil. Blend till smooth.
2. Warm up your Ninja Dual Zone Air Fryer to 200°C.
3. Put pita triangles in each cooking basket zone. Cook within five mins per side till crispy. Remove, then cool it down.
4. Drizzled beetroot hummus using oil, then serve with pita triangles.

Ingredients

250 grams cooked chickpeas - 200 grams beetroot, cooked & peeled - Two garlic cloves - 60 millilitres tahini paste - 45 millilitres lemon juice - 30 millilitres olive oil - Salt, as required - Four pita breads, sliced into triangles

NUTRITIONAL VALUES (PER SERVING): CALORIES: 410; CARBS: 55G; FAT: 16G; PROTEIN: 14G

Chorizo & Red Wine
Reduction Pots

🕐 **Prep:** *15* mins   🍲 **Cook:** *25* mins   🍽 **Serves:** *4*

Directions

1. Warm up your Ninja Dual Zone Air Fryer to 180°C.
2. In your pan on moderate temp, cook chorizo within five mins till browned. Remove, then put aside.
3. In your same pan, cook onion plus garlic till softened. Add cherry tomatoes, then cook within three mins, till soften.
4. Add red wine, adjust to high temp, let it simmer within five mins. Add cooked chorizo, then mix well.
5. Split mixture among four oven-safe pots, then place them on each cooking tray zone.
6. Cook within fifteen mins till bubbling. Flavour it using salt plus pepper, then serve.

Ingredients

400 grams chorizo, sliced
250 millilitres red wine
100 grams cherry tomatoes, halved
One big red onion, diced
Two garlic cloves, minced
Salt & pepper, as required

NUTRITIONAL VALUES (PER SERVING): CALORIES: 478; CARBS: 12G; FAT: 35G; PROTEIN: 24G

Vegan Lentil & Vegetable
Samosas

🕐 **Prep:** *15* mins   🍲 **Cook:** *20* mins   🍽 **Serves:** *4*

Directions

1. In your big container, mix cooked lentils, vegetables, potatoes, onion, juice, salt, pepper, cumin, plus coriander.
2. Warm up your ninja Dual Zone Air Fryer at 180°C.
3. Slice each filo pastry sheet in half lengthwise. Put some lentil mixture in each filo strip.
4. Fold pastry to create a triangle, then continue folding till finish. Brush edges using some water to seal.
5. Lightly brush each samosa using oil. Put samosas in each cooking basket zone.
6. Cook within ten mins side, flip each samosa, then cook within ten mins till crispy. Serve.

Ingredients

150 grams red lentils, cooked - 200 grams mixed vegetables, cooked - 150 grams potatoes, cooked & mashed - Eight vegan filo pastry sheets - 50 grams onion, finely chopped - 10 millilitres lemon juice - Five grams salt - Five grams black pepper - Five grams cumin, ground - Five grams coriander, ground

NUTRITIONAL VALUES (PER SERVING): CALORIES: 310; CARBS: 45G; FAT: 10G; PROTEIN: 12G

Brie & Cranberry
Tartlets

🕐 Prep: *20 mins* 📠 Cook: *10 mins* 🍽 Serves: *6*

Directions

1. Warm up your ninja Dual Zone Air Fryer to 200°C.
2. Put six pastry circles onto each cooking basket zone. Put cubed Brie onto each pastry circle.
3. Top it using some cranberry sauce plus dried cranberries. Put another pastry circle on each filled circle, pressing down to seal.
4. Slice a small slit on each tartlet, then cook within ten mins till golden. Serve.

Ingredients

200 grams puff pastry, rolled out & sliced into 12 circles - 150 grams Brie, cubed - 60g dried cranberries - 45 millilitres cranberry sauce - Flour for dusting

NUTRITIONAL VALUES (PER SERVING): CALORIES: 475; CARBS: 48G; FAT: 26G; PROTEIN: 13G

Goats Cheese Balls
With Chilli Jam

🕐 Prep: *15 mins* 📠 Cook: *10 mins* 🍽 Serves: *4*

Directions

1. Roll goat cheese into small balls.
2. In your shallow container, beat egg, salt plus pepper.
3. Put breadcrumbs in your second container dish, then flour in third. Coat each cheese ball in flour, dip in egg, then roll in breadcrumbs.
4. Warm up your Ninja Dual Zone Air Fryer to 200°C.
5. Put cheese balls in each greased cooking basket zone, then cook within ten mins till crispy, turning them once. Serve with chilli jam on top.

Ingredients

200 grams goats cheese, crumbled
50 grams panko breadcrumbs
One egg
50 grams plain flour
Salt & pepper, as required
100 millilitres chilli jam

NUTRITIONAL VALUES (PER SERVING): CALORIES: 375; CARBS: 30G; FAT: 20G; PROTEIN: 19G

Mini Welsh Rarebit
Toasties

🕐 **Prep:** *10* mins   📟 **Cook:** *8* mins   🍽 **Serves:** *4*

Directions

1. In your medium container, mix cheddar, milk, mustard, butter, plus egg.
2. Lay bread slices on your clean surface, then spread rarebit mixture on each bread slices. Put tomatoes on top.
3. Warm up your ninja Dual Zone Air Fryer to 180°C.
4. Put mini toasties in each cooking basket zone. Cook within four mins till crispy. Serve.

Ingredients

200 grams bread, sliced & sliced into eight quarters - 100 grams cheddar cheese, grated - 50 millilitres milk - 50 grams whole grain mustard - 25 grams butter, melted - One egg, beaten - 200 grams cherry tomatoes, halved

NUTRITIONAL VALUES (PER SERVING): CALORIES: 456; CARBS: 38G; FAT: 25G; PROTEIN: 19G

Seafood
& Avocado Cocktail

🕐 **Prep:** *15* mins   📟 **Cook:** *10* mins   🍽 **Serves:** *4*

Directions

1. Warm up your Ninja Dual Zone air fryer to 180°C.
2. Put mixed seafood in your cooking basket zone one, then cook within eight to ten mins till seafood is cooked, shaking once.
3. In your container, mix avocado, tomatoes, plus lettuce. Put aside.
4. In your small container, whisk mayonnaise, ketchup, plus juice. Flavour it using salt plus pepper.
5. Split avocado mixture among four glasses, then add seafood on top. Drizzle each using cocktail sauce. Serve.

Ingredients

300 grams mixed seafood - Two avocados, pitted and diced - 100 grams cherry tomatoes, halved - 50 grams lettuce, shredded - 100 millilitres mayonnaise - 30 millilitres tomato ketchup - 30 millilitres lemon juice - Salt & pepper, as required

NUTRITIONAL VALUES (PER SERVING): CALORIES: 392; CARBS: 17G; FAT: 30G; PROTEIN: 18G

Spinach & Ricotta
Stuffed Mushrooms

🕐 **Prep:** *15 mins*   🍲 **Cook:** *10 mins*   🍽 **Serves:** *4*

Directions

1. Warm up your ninja Dual Zone Air Fryer to 200°C.
2. In your medium container, mix spinach, ricotta, garlic, Parmesan, breadcrumbs, salt plus pepper.
3. Fill each mushroom cap with it, then put them in each cooking basket zone. Drizzle using oil. Cook within ten mins till golden brown. Serve.

Ingredients

200 grams spinach, washed & chopped
150 grams ricotta cheese
Twelve mushrooms, stems removed
Six grams garlic, minced
50 grams Parmesan cheese, grated
30 grams breadcrumbs
20 millilitres olive oil

NUTRITIONAL VALUES (PER SERVING): CALORIES: 280; CARBS: 17G; FAT: 16G; PROTEIN: 21G

Smoked Salmon
& Cream Cheese Blinis

🕐 **Prep:** *15 mins*   🍲 **Cook:** *8 mins*   🍽 **Serves:** *4*

Directions

1. In your container, mix flour, milk, plus egg till smooth.
2. Warm up your ninja Dual Zone Air Fryer at 180°C.
3. Pour some blini batter onto each cooking basket zone, creating small round blinis.
4. Cook within four mins per side, flip, then cook within four mins till golden. Remove, cool it down, then put aside.
5. In your separate container, mix cream cheese plus juice. Flavour it using salt plus pepper. Spread it onto each cooked blini.
6. Top each blini using smoked salmon slice. Serve.

Ingredients

100 grams plain flour
One litre whole milk
One big egg
200 grams smoked salmon slices
150 grams cream cheese
30 millilitres fresh lemon juice
Salt & pepper, as required

NUTRITIONAL VALUES (PER SERVING): CALORIES: 425; CARBS: 38G; FAT: 20G; PROTEIN: 25G

Mini Ploughman's
Bites

🕐 **Prep:** *15* mins   📠 **Cook:** *10* mins   🍽 **Serves:** *4*

Directions

1. Warm up your ninja Dual Zone Air Fryer to 190°C.
2. In your big container, mix bread, cheese, tomatoes, plus ham. Drizzle oil, then flavour it using salt plus pepper. Toss well.
3. Split it into each cooking basket zone, then cook within ten mins, till crispy, shaking once. Serve.

Ingredients

200 grams crusty bread, bite-sized
100 grams cheddar cheese, small cubes
One kilogram cherry tomatoes
200 grams cooked ham, diced
100 millilitres olive oil
Salt & pepper, as required

NUTRITIONAL VALUES (PER SERVING): CALORIES: 480; CARBS: 48G; FAT: 22G; PROTEIN: 28G

Curried Lentil
& Vegetable Soup

🕐 **Prep:** *15* mins   📠 **Cook:** *30* mins   🍽 **Serves:** *4*

Directions

1. Warm up your Ninja Dual Zone Air Fryer at 200°C to "Roast" function.
2. Put vegetables, onion, plus garlic in your cooking basket zone one, then cook within ten mins.
3. Warm up 30 millilitres oil in your cooking basket zone two, then add curry powder. Mix till a past form within two mins. Add lentils, then mix well.
4. Add cooked vegetables, plus broth, then flavour it using salt plus pepper. Mix well.
5. Adjust on "High" at 180°C within twenty mins till lentils are tender. Once cooked, mix in coconut milk, then serve.

Ingredients

200 grams dried green lentils, washed & strained - 250 grams mixed vegetables, chopped - One big onion, chopped - Two garlic cloves, minced - 25 grams curry powder - One & half litres vegetable broth - 200 millilitres coconut milk - Salt & pepper, as required

NUTRITIONAL VALUES (PER SERVING): CALORIES: 350; CARBS: 54G; FAT: 9G; PROTEIN: 18G

Crispy Whitebait
With Tartar Sauce

 **Prep:** *15 mins*  **Cook:** *10 mins* **Serves:** *4*

Directions

1. Warm up your ninja Dual Zone air fryer to 200°C.
2. In your big container, mix flour, salt, plus pepper. Add whitebait, then mix well.
3. Put coated whitebait to your greased cooking basket. Cook within ten mins, flipping once.
4. Mix mayonnaise, capers, gherkins, plus juice in your small container. Serve cooked whitebait with tartar sauce.

Ingredients

500 grams whitebait - 150 grams plain flour - Two grams each salt & black pepper

For the Tartar Sauce:
150 millilitres mayonnaise - 30 millilitres capers, strained & chopped - 30 millilitres gherkins, chopped - 20 millilitres lemon juice

NUTRITIONAL VALUES (PER SERVING): CALORIES: 482; CARBS: 38G; FAT: 24G; PROTEIN: 31G

Devilled Eggs
With Smoked Paprika

 **Prep:** *15 mins*  **Cook:** *16 mins* **Serves:** *6*

Directions

1. Warm up your Ninja Dual Zone Air Fryer to 120°C.
2. Split eggs in each cooking basket zone, then cook within sixteen mins. Remove, cool it down, peel, then slice into half lengthwise.
3. Take yolks from each egg half, then put them in your container. Add mayonnaise, mustard, paprika, salt, plus pepper. Mix well. Fill each egg white half with it. Serve.

Ingredients

Twelve big eggs
75 millilitres mayonnaise
30 grams Dijon mustard
10 grams smoked paprika
Two grams each salt & ground black pepper

NUTRITIONAL VALUES (PER SERVING): CALORIES: 185; CARBS: 1G; FAT: 15G; PROTEIN: 12G

Mini Beef
& Horseradish Yorkshires

🕐 **Prep:** *15 mins*   ▦ **Cook:** *20 mins*   🍽 **Serves:** *12*

Directions

1. In your medium container, mix flour, eggs, plus milk. Flavour it using salt plus pepper.
2. Warm up your ninja Dual Zone Air Fryer to 200°C.
3. Put five millilitres oil into each 12-silicone muffin tray hole, then put it in your cooking basket zone one to warm up.
4. Take hot tray, then add batter into each hole. Put in your cooking basket, then cook within twelve to fifteen mins. Remove, then cool it down.
5. Put some horseradish sauce onto each Yorkshire, plus roast beef slice on top. Serve.

Ingredients

100 grams flour, plain
Two big eggs
150 millilitres milk
Salt & pepper, as required
25 grams beef dripping or vegetable oil
200 grams roast beef, thinly sliced
50 grams horseradish sauce

NUTRITIONAL VALUES (PER SERVING): CALORIES: 110; CARBS: 9.2G; FAT: 4.1G; PROTEIN: 7.4G

Tomato & Mozzarella
Bruschettas

🕐 **Prep:** *10 mins*   ▦ **Cook:** *5 mins*   🍽 **Serves:** *4*

Directions

1. Warm up your ninja Dual Zone Air Fryer to 200°C.
2. In your small container, mix cherry tomatoes plus garlic. Flavour it using salt plus pepper.
3. Put bread slices in your cooking basket zone one, then drizzle them using oil.
4. Cook bread slices within two mins, flip them over, then cook within two mins till golden.
5. Remove your bread, then put tomato mixture on each slice. Add some mozzarella on top.
6. Put bruschettas to your cooking basket, then cook within one min till warmed. Sprinkle basil on top, then serve.

Ingredients

250 grams cherry tomatoes, halved
200 grams fresh mozzarella, sliced
Four rustic bread slices
30 millilitres olive oil
Six grams cloves garlic, minced
20 grams basil leaves, chopped
Salt & pepper, as required

NUTRITIONAL VALUES (PER SERVING): CALORIES 280; CARBS 18G; FAT 16G; PROTEIN 12G

Potted Shrimp
With Melba Toast

🕐 **Prep:** *15 mins* 📖 **Cook:** *5 mins* 🍽 **Serves:** *4*

Directions

1. In your saucepan, dissolve butter on low temp. Add ground mace, cayenne, Worcestershire, plus juice, then mix well.
2. Add shrimp, then cook within three to four mins till cooked. Warm up your Ninja Dual Zone Air Fryer to 175°C.
3. Put bread pieces into each cooking basket zone. Cook within five mins till crisp. Serve with shrimp.

Ingredients

300 grams shrimp, peeled & cleaned - 100 grams unsalted butter - Two millilitres ground mace - Three millilitres cayenne pepper - Two millilitres Worcestershire sauce - 45 millilitres lemon juice - Eight white bread slices, crusts removed, flattened & sliced into four

NUTRITIONAL VALUES (PER SERVING): CALORIES: 405; CARBS: 29G; FAT: 23G; PROTEIN: 22G

Stilton & Walnut
Stuffed Figs

🕐 **Prep:** *15 mins* 📖 **Cook:** *10 mins* 🍽 **Serves:** *4*

Directions

1. Warm up your ninja Dual Zone Air Fryer to 180°C.
2. Stuff each fig with some stilton cheese, put them in each cooking basket zone. Cook within ten mins till figs become tender.
3. Mix walnuts plus honey in your small container. Drizzle cooked figs with honey-walnut mixture, then sprinkle black pepper on top. Serve.

Ingredients

Twelve fresh figs, sliced X-shaped on each
150 grams stilton cheese, crumbled
60 grams walnuts, chopped
30 millilitres honey
Ground black pepper, as required

NUTRITIONAL VALUES (PER SERVING): CALORIES: 365; CARBS: 45G; FAT: 18G; PROTEIN: 10G

Ham Hock
& Pea Terrine

 **Prep:** *20 mins*    **Cook:** *2 h*   **Serves:** *6*

Directions

1. In your big container, mix ham hock, split peas, mustard, thyme, plus vinegar. Flavour it using salt plus pepper.
2. Warm up your ninja Dual Zone Air Fryer to 180°C.
3. Pour stock on powdered gelatine, then whisk quickly till dissolved. Cool it slightly.
4. Pour half of gelatine mixture into your greased terrine mould. Press ham hock-pea mixture on top.
5. Pour rest of gelatine mixture on ham hock-pea mixture.
6. Put terrine mould or loaf tin into your cooking basket zone one, then cook within two hours till firm. Remove, cool it down, then chill in your fridge within four hours. Slice, then serve.

Ingredients

One kilograms ham hock, deboned & shredded - 300 grams split peas, cooked - 30 grams whole grain mustard - Six grams fresh thyme leaves - 60 millilitres apple cider vinegar - Salt & pepper, as required - 50 millilitres vegetable oil - 20 grams powdered gelatine - 250 millilitres hot chicken stock

NUTRITIONAL VALUES (PER SERVING): CALORIES: 500; CARBS: 38G; FAT: 22G; PROTEIN: 42G

Mackerel Pâté
With Cucumber Pickle

 **Prep:** *15 mins*    **Cook:** *10 mins*   **Serves:** *4*

Directions

1. Warm up your Ninja Dual Zone Air Fryer to 180°C.
2. Flavour mackerel fillets using salt plus pepper. Put them in your cooking basket zone one, then cook within ten mins, till cooked.
3. Meanwhile, mix cucumber, wine vinegar plus sugar in your small container. Put aside.
4. Remove cooked mackerel fillets, then cool it down.
5. In your food processor, mix cooled mackerel, cream cheese, sour cream, butter, zest, plus lemon juice. Blend till smooth. Flavour it using salt plus pepper.
6. Serve mackerel pâté with cucumber pickle.

Ingredients

400 grams mackerel fillets, skin removed - 150 grams cream cheese - 100 millilitres sour cream - 50 grams butter, melted - One lemon, zest & 30 millilitres juice - Salt & pepper, as required
For the Cucumber Pickle:
200 grams cucumber, thinly sliced - 50 millilitres white wine vinegar - 25 grams sugar

NUTRITIONAL VALUES (PER SERVING): CALORIES: 710; CARBS: 12G; FAT: 63G; PROTEIN: 28G

Watermelon & Feta
Skewers

🕐 **Prep:** *10 mins* 📱 **Cook:** *5 mins* 🍽 **Serves:** *4*

Directions

1. Warm up your ninja Dual Zone Air Fryer to 180°C.
2. Thread watermelon plus feta cheese onto each skewer.
3. In your small container, mix oil, mint, plus pepper.
4. Put skewers in your cooking basket zone one, then cook within five mins, turning once. Serve it with mint-infused olive oil mixture on top.

Ingredients

500 grams watermelon cubes
200 grams feta cheese cubes
50 millilitres olive oil
20 grams mint leaves, chopped
Two grams black pepper, ground

NUTRITIONAL VALUES (PER SERVING): CALORIES: 395; CARBS: 15G; FAT: 32G; PROTEIN: 10G

Spicy Lamb Koftas
With Yogurt Dip

🕐 **Prep:** *15 mins* 📱 **Cook:** *15 mins* 🍽 **Serves:** *4*

Directions

1. In your big container, mix lamb, breadcrumbs, onions, coriander, garlic, cumin, paprika, salt, and pepper. Form it into eight elongated kofta.
2. Warm up your ninja Dual Zone Air Fryer to 190°C.
3. Put lamb koftas in each greased cooking basket zone, then cook within thirteen to fifteen mins, turning once.
4. Meanwhile, mix yogurt, mint, zest, juice, salt, plus pepper in your small container. Serve cooked koftas with it.

Ingredients

500 grams minced lamb - 100 grams breadcrumbs - 60 grams onion, chopped - 30 grams fresh coriander, chopped - 9 grams garlic, minced - 15 grams ground cumin - 15 grams ground paprika - Salt & pepper, as required
For the yogurt dip:
250 millilitres Greek yogurt - 20 grams fresh mint leaves, chopped - Zest & 30 millilitres juice of half a lemon - Salt & pepper, as required

NUTRITIONAL VALUES (PER SERVING): CALORIES: 450; CARBS: 29G; FAT: 25G; PROTEIN: 30G

Vegetarian Scotch
Quail Eggs

🕐 **Prep:** *15 mins*　　📟 **Cook:** *15 mins*　　🍽 **Serves:** *4*

Directions

1. Split meat-free sausage into twelve, then flatten each into circles. Put quail egg in each, then wrap sausage around it to seal.
2. Put flour in first container, beaten eggs in second, then put breadcrumbs on third.
3. Roll each sausage-wrapped quail egg in flour, dip it in egg, then roll it in breadcrumbs.
4. Warm up your ninja Dual Zone air fryer to 180°C. Put breaded quail eggs in each cooking basket zone.
5. Cook within fifteen mins till crispy, turning them once. Serve.

Ingredients

12 quail eggs, boiled & peeled
400 grams meat-free sausage or vegetarian haggis
50 grams plain flour
Two big beaten eggs
100 grams breadcrumbs

NUTRITIONAL VALUES (PER SERVING): CALORIES: 450; CARBS: 40G; FAT: 20G; PROTEIN: 24G

Prawn & Chorizo
Skewers

🕐 **Prep:** *10 mins*　　📟 **Cook:** *8 mins*　　🍽 **Serves:** *4*

Directions

1. In your big container, mix prawns, chorizo, oil, bell peppers, paprika, salt, plus black pepper. Thread it onto skewers.
2. Warm up your ninja Dual Zone Air Fryer to 200°C.
3. Put skewers in each cooking basket zone, then cook within eight mins, flipping once. Serve.

Ingredients

500 grams raw prawns, peeled & cleaned
200 grams chorizo, sliced into thin rounds
100 millilitres olive oil
50 grams diced each yellow & red bell pepper
Two grams each paprika, salt & black pepper

NUTRITIONAL VALUES (PER SERVING): CALORIES: 470; CARBS: 4G; FAT: 35G; PROTEIN: 34G

Dauphinoise Potatoes
With Garlic & Cream

 **Prep:** *20 mins*    **Cook:** *45 mins*   **Serves:** *4*

Directions

1. In your big container, mix potatoes, garlic, double cream, salt, plus pepper.
2. Warm up your ninja Dual Zone Air Fryer to 200°C. Put potato slices in each cooking basket zone. Pour any excess cream mixture.
3. Cook within thirty mins, sprinkle Gruyere cheese on top, then cook again within fifteen mins till cooked. Serve.

Ingredients

One kilogram potatoes, peeled & sliced thinly
Three cloves garlic, minced
500 millilitres double cream
Salt & black pepper, as required
50 grams grated Gruyere cheese

NUTRITIONAL VALUES (PER SERVING): CALORIES: 580; CARBS: 43G; FAT: 38G; PROTEIN: 15G

Braised Red Cabbage
With Apples

 **Prep:** *15 mins*   **Cook:** *45 mins*   **Serves:** *4*

Directions

1. Warm up your ninja Dual Zone Air Fryer to 180°C.
2. In your big container, mix red cabbage, apples, plus onion.
3. In your separate container, mix apple cider, sugar, plus stock. Pour vinegar mixture on cabbage mixture, then flavour it using salt plus pepper.
4. Split mixture in each cooking basket zone, the cook within into the air fryer basket forty-five mins, mixing twice. Serve.

Ingredients

One kilogram red cabbage, thinly sliced -
300 grams medium apples, peeled & thinly sliced
- 100 grams onion, finely chopped - 150 millilitres
apple cider vinegar - 50 grams light brown sugar -
200 millilitres vegetable stock - Salt & pepper, as
required

NUTRITIONAL VALUES (PER SERVING): CALORIES: 210; CARBS: 38G; FAT: 5G; PROTEIN: 3G

Air-Fried
Hasselback Potatoes

🕐 **Prep:** *15 mins*   ▦ **Cook:** *40 mins*   🍽 **Serves:** *4*

Directions

1. Warm up your ninja Dual Zone Air Fryer to 200°C.
2. In your small container, mix salt, pepper, paprika, powdered garlic, plus powdered onion.
3. Brush each potato using oil, then sprinkle seasoning on top.
4. Put potatoes in each cooking basket zone, then cook within forty mins till crispy. Serve.

Ingredients

800 grams medium potatoes, sliced thin along width of each potato, stopping half-centimetre from bottom - 30 millilitres olive oil - Two grams each salt & black pepper - Five grams each paprika, powdered garlic & powdered onion

NUTRITIONAL VALUES (PER SERVING): CALORIES: 210; CARBS: 38G; FAT: 5G; PROTEIN: 5G

Roasted Root
Vegetables with Thyme

🕐 **Prep:** *15 mins*   ▦ **Cook:** *20 mins*   🍽 **Serves:** *4*

Directions

1. Warm up your Ninja Dual Zone Air Fryer to 200°C.
2. In your big container, mix carrots, parsnips, beetroot, plus sweet potatoes. Drizzle using oil, then sprinkle thyme on top. Mix well.
3. Flavour it using salt plus pepper. Put vegetable mixture in each cooking basket zone. Cook within twenty mins, shaking them once. Serve.

Ingredients

300 grams each carrots & parsnips, peeled & chunks
200 grams each beetroot & sweet potatoes, peeled & chunks
30 millilitres olive oil
Four grams fresh thyme, chopped
Salt & pepper, as required

NUTRITIONAL VALUES (PER SERVING): CALORIES: 289; CARBS: 46G; FAT: 10G; PROTEIN: 4G

Minted Pea
& Broad Bean Mash

🕐 **Prep:** *15 mins*   📷 **Cook:** *15 mins*   🍽 **Serves:** *4*

Directions

1. Arrange peas and broad beans in your cooking basket zone one, then add stock on top.
2. Set your air fryer to "Steam" at 200°C, then cook within ten mins till tender.
3. Transfer them into your big container, then add mint, salt, pepper, plus oil. Mash till smooth before serving.

Ingredients

500 grams each peas & broad beans
100 millilitres vegetable stock
One bunch of fresh mint leaves, finely chopped
Salt & pepper, as required
50 millilitres olive oil

NUTRITIONAL VALUES (PER SERVING): CALORIES: 260; CARBS: 32G; FAT: 11G; PROTEIN: 12G

Garlic & Rosemary
Focaccia Bread

🕐 **Prep:** *15 mins*   📷 **Cook:** *20 mins*   🍽 **Serves:** *6*

Directions

1. In your big container, mix flour, yeast, plus salt. Add lukewarm water, then mix till a soft dough forms.
2. Knead it on your lightly floured surface within five mins, till elastic.
3. Transfer it to your oiled container, cover, then let it rise within one hour, till doubled in size.
4. Warm up your Ninja Dual Zone air fryer to 200°C.
5. Stretch, then shape your dough into a rectangle. Dimple dough surface using your finger, then drizzle oil on top.
6. Sprinkle garlic plus rosemary, then put it to lined cooking tray. Cook within twenty mins till golden. Remove, cool it down, slice, then serve.

Ingredients

500 grams white bread flour, strong - Seven grams dried yeast, fast-action - Five grams fine sea salt - 300 millilitres lukewarm water - 75 millilitres olive oil - Three cloves garlic, chopped - Two fresh rosemary sprigs, chopped

NUTRITIONAL VALUES (PER SERVING): CALORIES: 432; CARBS: 64G; FAT: 14G; PROTEIN: 10G

Creamy Leek
& Potato Gratin

Prep: *15 mins*　　**Cook:** *40 mins*　　**Serves:** *4*

Directions

1. Mix double cream, milk, garlic, salt, plus pepper in your big container. Add potatoes, then mix well.
2. Warm up your ninja Dual Zone Air Fryer to 180°C.
3. Cook leeks in your pan on moderate temp within five mins till softened. Layer half of sautéed leeks in your baking dish.
4. Put half of potato slices on top, another leeks layer plus rest of potato slices. Add any excess cream mixture on top.
5. Put baking dish into your cooking basket zone one, the cook within thirty mins.
6. Remove dish, add Cheddar, then cook within ten mins till golden. Serve.

Ingredients

500 grams potatoes, peeled & sliced
300 grams leeks, trimmed, sliced & washed
200 millilitres double cream
100 millilitres milk
Two garlic cloves, minced
100 grams Cheddar cheese, grated
Salt & pepper, as required

NUTRITIONAL VALUES (PER SERVING): CALORIES 445; CARBS 34G; FAT 31G; PROTEIN 12G

Beer-Battered
Onion Rings

Prep: *15 mins*　　**Cook:** *15 mins*　　**Serves:** *4*

Directions

1. In your big container, mix flour plus beer till smooth. Toss onion rings plus cornstarch in your separate container.
2. Warm up your Ninja Dual Zone Air Fryer to 180°C.
3. Coat each onion ring into beer batter, then put them in each cooking basket zone. Cook within ten mins, till crispy, flipping once.
4. Remove, strain excess oil, cook it down, then flavour it using salt. Serve.

Ingredients

200 grams flour, all-purpose
200 millilitres UK lager beer
One kilogram onions, sliced into rings
500 millilitres sunflower oil
Salt, as required
100 grams cornstarch

NUTRITIONAL VALUES (PER SERVING): CALORIES: 670; CARBS: 119G; FAT: 17G; PROTEIN: 14G

Honey Roasted
Parsnips & Carrots

🕐 **Prep:** *10 mins*　📠 **Cook:** *20 mins*　🍽 **Serves:** *4*

Directions

1. Warm up your ninja Dual Zone Air Fryer to 180°C.
2. In your big container, mix parsnips, carrots, oil, honey, salt, pepper, plus rosemary.
3. Put vegetable mixture in each cooking basket zone, then cook within twenty mins till golden brown, swapping basket once. Serve.

Ingredients

400 grams parsnips, peeled & quartered - 400 grams carrots, peeled & sliced into thick strips - 30 millilitres olive oil - 60 millilitres honey - Two grams each salt & dried rosemary - One gram black pepper, ground

NUTRITIONAL VALUES (PER SERVING): CALORIES: 270; CARBS: 45G; FAT: 9G; PROTEIN: 3G

Mixed Greens
With Lemon Butter Sauce

🕐 **Prep:** *10 mins*　📠 **Cook:** *15 mins*　🍽 **Serves:** *4*

Directions

1. Warm up your ninja Dual Zone Air Fryer to 180°C.
2. In your big container, mix greens, tomatoes, lemon juice, butter, plus oil. Flavour it using salt plus pepper.
3. Divide it in each cooking basket zone, then cook within seven mins, switch basket, then cook within seven mins. Serve with Parmesan cheese.

Ingredients

200 grams mixed greens - 100 grams cherry tomatoes, halved - 50 millilitres lemon juice - 100 grams unsalted butter, dissolved - 30 millilitres olive oil - Salt & pepper, as required - 50 grams grated Parmesan cheese

NUTRITIONAL VALUES (PER SERVING): CALORIES: 320; CARBS: 8G; FAT: 28G; PROTEIN: 9G

Spicy Bombay
Potatoes

🕐 **Prep:** *15* mins   🍲 **Cook:** *30* mins   🍽 **Serves:** *4*

Directions

1. Warm up oil in your skillet on moderate temp. Add mustard seeds plus cumin seeds, then cook till it starts to pop.
2. Mix in baby potatoes, turmeric powder, chili powder, plus garam masala.
3. Warm up your Ninja Dual Zone Air Fryer to 180°C.
4. Put spice-coated potatoes, onions, garlic, plus ginger in each cooking basket zone. Cook within thirty mins till crispy, tossing once. Serve.

Ingredients

800 grams of baby potatoes, halved & boiled - 30 millilitres vegetable oil - Two grams each mustard seeds & cumin seeds - One gram turmeric powder - Two grams each chili powder & garam masala - 200 grams onion, chopped - 10 grams garlic, minced - 10 grams ginger, minced

NUTRITIONAL VALUES (PER SERVING): CALORIES: 260; CARBS: 47G; FAT: 6G; PROTEIN: 6G

Caramelised Brussel Sprouts
With Chestnuts

🕐 **Prep:** *15* mins   🍲 **Cook:** *20* mins   🍽 **Serves:** *4*

Directions

1. In your big container, mix Brussel sprouts, chestnuts, oil, butter, sugar, sea salt, plus black pepper.
2. Warm up your Ninja Dual Zone Air Fryer to 180°C.
3. Split Brussel sprout-chestnut mixture between both cooking basket zones.
4. Cook within ten mins, swap basket, then cook within ten mins till tender. Serve.

Ingredients

500 grams Brussel sprouts, trimmed & halved
200 grams chestnuts, cooked & peeled
30 millilitres olive oil
30 grams unsalted butter, melted
10 grams light brown sugar
Two grams sea salt
Ground black pepper, as required

NUTRITIONAL VALUES (PER SERVING): CALORIES: 310; CARBS: 35G; FAT: 17G; PROTEIN: 7G

Yorkshire Puddings
With Chive Butter

🕐 **Prep:** *15 mins*   📱 **Cook:** *20 mins*   🍽 **Serves:** *4*

Directions

1. In your big container, mix flour, eggs, milk, plus butter till smooth. Flavour it using salt plus pepper. Put aside within fifteen mins.
2. Warm up your Ninja Dual Zone Air Fryer to 200°C.
3. In your small container, mix chives plus butter till blended. Put aside.
4. Oil four small ramekins using some chive butter. Pour batter into each ramekin, then move them in each cooking basket zone.
5. Cook within twenty mins till golden brown. Remove, cool it down, then serve with chive butter on top.

Ingredients

200 grams plain flour
Four big eggs
300 millilitres whole milk
50 grams unsalted butter, dissolved
Salt & pepper, as required
100 grams chives, chopped
150 grams unsalted butter, softened

NUTRITIONAL VALUES (PER SERVING): CALORIES: 650; CARBS: 42G; FAT: 46G; PROTEIN: 18G

Balsamic Glazed Beetroot
& Goats Cheese Salad

🕐 **Prep:** *15 mins*   📱 **Cook:** *25 mins*   🍽 **Serves:** *4*

Directions

1. Warm up your ninja Dual Zone Air Fryer to 200°C.
2. In your container, mix beetroot, salt, pepper, plus 15 millilitres oil.
3. Put beetroot in your cooking basket zone one, then cook within twenty-five mins till tender, shaking once. Remove, then cool it down.
4. meanwhile, whisk excess oil plus vinegar in your small container.
5. In your big container, mix salad leaves plus half of balsamic glaze.
6. Split salad leaves onto four plates. Top each plate with beetroot, goats cheese plus walnuts. Drizzle each with excess balsamic glaze. Serve.

Ingredients

800 grams beetroot, peeled & wedges - 200 grams soft goats cheese, crumbled - 100 grams mixed salad leaves - 50 grams walnuts, roughly chopped - Two grams each salt & black pepper - 30 millilitres olive oil - 60 millilitres balsamic vinegar

NUTRITIONAL VALUES (PER SERVING): CALORIES: 398; CARBS: 26G; FAT: 26G; PROTEIN: 13G

Creamed Spinach
With Nutmeg

🕐 **Prep:** *10 mins*　📠 **Cook:** *15 mins*　🍽 **Serves:** *4*

Directions

1. Warm up your ninja Dual Zone Air Fryer to 175°C.
2. Put butter, onion, plus garlic in your cooking basket zone one. Cook within five mins.
3. Meanwhile, put spinach leaves in your zone two cooking basket, then cook within three to four mins, till wilted.
4. Mix wilted spinach plus onion mixture in your cooking basket zone one. Pour heavy cream, then mix gently.
5. Sprinkle Parmesan cheese, then add ground nutmeg. Flavour it using salt plus pepper. Cook within six to eight mins till cheese is dissolved. Serve.

Ingredients

600 grams spinach leaves - 30 grams unsalted butter - 50 grams onion, chopped - Three grams garlic clove, minced - 200 millilitres heavy cream - 50 grams grated Parmesan cheese - 0.5 gram ground nutmeg - Salt & pepper, as required

NUTRITIONAL VALUES (PER SERVING): CALORIES: 350; CARBS: 10G; FAT: 28G; PROTEIN: 10G

Air-Fried Garlic
& Parsley Mushrooms

🕐 **Prep:** *10 mins*　📠 **Cook:** *8 mins*　🍽 **Serves:** *4*

Directions

1. In your big container, mix mushrooms, oil, garlic, salt, plus pepper.
2. Warm up your ninja Dual Zone Air Fryer to 175°C.
3. Put seasoned mushrooms in each cooking basket zone, then cook within eight mins, shaking once. Sprinkle with parsley, then serve.

Ingredients

400 grams mushrooms, cleaned & halved
30 millilitres olive oil
Four grams minced garlic
15 grams chopped fresh parsley
Salt & pepper, as required

NUTRITIONAL VALUES (PER SERVING): CALORIES: 91; CARBS: 4G; FAT: 7G; PROTEIN: 3G

Triple Cooked
Chunky Chips

🕐 **Prep:** *15 mins*   📦 **Cook:** *45 mins*   🍽 **Serves:** *4*

Directions

1. Warm up your Ninja Dual Zone Air Fryer to 160°C. Toss chips plus 15 millilitres oil in your container.
2. Transfer it to each cooking basket zone, then cook within twenty mins, shaking once.
3. Adjust to 180°C, then cook within twenty mins, shaking once. Adjust to 200°C, then cook within five mins. Remove chips, flavour it using salt, then serve.

Ingredients

1 kilogram Maris Piper potatoes, sliced into chunky chips, soaked withing ten mins, strained & pat dried - 30 millilitres vegetable oil - Salt, as required

NUTRITIONAL VALUES (PER SERVING): CALORIES: 350; CARBS: 48G; FAT: 15G; PROTEIN: 6G

Warm Couscous Salad
With Roasted Vegetables

🕐 **Prep:** *15 mins*   📦 **Cook:** *25 mins*   🍽 **Serves:** *4*

Directions

1. Warm up your ninja Dual Zone air fryer to 200°C.
2. Put assorted vegetables in your big container. Add garlic, zest, juice, plus 30 millilitres oil. Mix well.
3. Put vegetable mixture into each cooking basket zone, then cook within twenty mins till tender.
4. Meanwhile, warm up stock in your saucepan till boiling.
5. Put couscous in your heatproof container, then pour in stock. Cover, then let it sit within five mins. Fluff it
6. Remove cooked vegetables, then cool them down. Mix vegetables, cooked couscous, salt, pepper, feta plus basil leaves. Drizzle 15 millilitres oil, then mix well. Serve.

Ingredients

200 grams couscous - 500 millilitres vegetable stock - 400 grams assorted vegetables, chopped - Two garlic cloves, minced - One lemon, zest & juice - 45 millilitres olive oil - 50 grams feta cheese, crumbled - Salt & pepper, as required - 30 grams fresh basil leaves, chopped

NUTRITIONAL VALUES (PER SERVING): CALORIES: 319; CARBS: 40G; FAT: 13G; PROTEIN: 10G

Crunchy
Cauliflower Cheese

🕐 **Prep:** *10* mins ⬛ **Cook:** *20* mins 🍽 **Serves:** *4*

Directions

1. Warm up your ninja Dual Zone air fryer to 180°C.
2. In your saucepan, dissolve butter on moderate temp. Add flour, then cook within one min, mixing.
3. Whisk in milk till smooth within two mins. Remove saucepan, then mix in half of cheddar. Flavour it using salt plus pepper.
4. In your big container, mix cauliflower plus cheese sauce. Split cauliflower mixture in each cooking basket zone.
5. In your small container, mix excess cheddar plus breadcrumbs. Sprinkle it on cauliflower. Cook within twenty mins till golden. Serve.

Ingredients

One kilogram cauliflower florets
100 grams cheddar cheese, grated
300 millilitres whole milk
50 grams all-purpose flour
50 grams butter
100 grams fresh breadcrumbs
Salt & pepper, as required

NUTRITIONAL VALUES (PER SERVING): CALORIES: 460; CARBS: 38G; FAT: 25G; PROTEIN: 17G

Buttered New
Potatoes with Dill

🕐 **Prep:** *10* mins ⬛ **Cook:** *15* mins 🍽 **Serves:** *4*

Directions

1. In your container, mix butter, oil, salt, plus pepper. Add potatoes, then mix well.
2. Warm up your Ninja Dual Zone Air Fryer to 190°C. Put coated new potatoes in each cooking basket zone.
3. Cook within fifteen mins till golden, shaking once. Remove, cool it down, then sprinkle dill on top. Serve.

Ingredients

800 grams new potatoes, halved
30 grams unsalted butter, dissolved
15 millilitres olive oil
10 grams fresh dill, chopped
Salt & pepper, as required

NUTRITIONAL VALUES (PER SERVING): CALORIES: 266; CARBS: 34G; FAT: 13G; PROTEIN: 4G

Vegan "Beef" Wellington

🕐 Prep: *30* mins   🍲 Cook: *40* mins   🍽 Serves: *4*

Ingredients

Directions

1. In your big pan, warm up oil on moderate temp. Put onions, then cook till soft.
2. Put mushrooms, garlic, plus thyme. Cook till mushrooms reduced in size.
3. Mix in vegan "beef" mince plus soy sauce. Flavour it using salt plus pepper. Add stock, then simmer within ten mins.
4. Warm up your Ninja Dual Zone Air Fryer to 190°C.
5. Spread "beef" mixture in pastry centre, fold to half, then press edges to seal.
6. Put your wellington to your lined cooking basket zone one. Brush wellington top using milk. Cook within forty mins till golden brown. Serve.

450 grams vegan "beef" mince - 200 grams chestnut mushrooms, chopped - One big onion, chopped - Three garlic cloves, minced - 200 millilitres vegetable stock - 15 millilitres olive oil - 10 grams thyme leaves - 30 millilitres soy sauce - Salt & pepper, as required - 320 grams vegan puff pastry, ready-made, rolled out - 80 millilitres plant-based milk

NUTRITIONAL VALUES (PER SERVING): CALORIES: 760; CARBS: 66G; FAT: 44G; PROTEIN: 23G

Air-Fried Spiced Tofu Steaks

🕐 Prep: *15* mins   🍲 Cook: *12* mins   🍽 Serves: *4*

Ingredients

Directions

1. In your shallow container, whisk soy sauce, oil, juice, paprika, oregano, powdered garlic, cumin, salt, plus pepper. Add tofu steaks, then marinate within ten mins.
2. Warm up your Ninja Dual Zone Air Fryer at 200°C. Put marinated tofu steaks in each cooking basket zone.
3. Cook within twelve mins per side, flipping once. Serve.

400 grams firm tofu, pressed & sliced into one cm thick steaks - 60 millilitres soy sauce - 30 millilitres olive oil - 50 millilitres lemon juice - Three grams each smoked paprika & powdered garlic - One gram each dried oregano & ground cumin - Salt & pepper, as required

NUTRITIONAL VALUES (PER SERVING): CALORIES: 226; CARBS: 5G; FAT: 18G; PROTEIN: 16G

Vegetable & Lentil
Curry Pots

🕐 **Prep:** *15 mins*   📟 **Cook:** *30 mins*   🍽 **Serves:** *4*

Directions

1. Warm your Ninja Dual Zone Air Fryer to 180°C.
2. In your big pan on moderate temp, add oil, then cook onion, garlic, plus ginger till fragrant.
3. Mix in curry powder, red lentils plus vegetables. Pour in stock, then flavour it using salt plus pepper.
4. Put this vegetable mixture in your heat-proof ramekins. Put ramekins in each cooking basket zone, then cook within fifteen mins.
5. Mix in coconut milk, then cook within fifteen mins. Serve.

Ingredients

300 grams mixed vegetables, chopped - 150 grams red lentils, washed & strained - One litre vegetable stock - 30 millilitres olive oil - 300 millilitres coconut milk - One onion, chopped - Two cloves garlic, minced - 15 grams fresh ginger, grated - Five grams curry powder- Salt & pepper, as required

NUTRITIONAL VALUES (PER SERVING): CALORIES: 372; CARBS: 41G; FAT: 18G; PROTEIN: 13G

Vegan "Chicken"
Nuggets with Dips

🕐 **Prep:** *15 mins*   📟 **Cook:** *20 mins*   🍽 **Serves:** *4*

Directions

1. Warm up your Ninja Dual Zone Air Fryer to 200°C.
2. In your container, mix flour, salt, plus pepper.
3. Pour milk into your separate container, then put breadcrumbs in third container.
4. Dip each vegan chicken-style piece into flour, then in milk, then coat using breadcrumbs.
5. Put breaded "chicken" nuggets on each cooking basket zone, then spray them using oil spray.
6. Cook within ten mins, flip them, then cook within ten mins till crispy.
7. In your small container, mix sweet chilli sauce plus water till blended.
8. In another small container, mix mayonnaise plus barbecue sauce till smooth.
9. Serve "chicken" nuggets with sweet chilli plus creamy BBQ dips.

Ingredients

300 grams vegan chicken-style pieces - 100 grams flour - 120 millilitres unsweetened almond milk - 150 grams breadcrumbs - Two grams salt - One gram black pepper

For Sweet Chilli Dip:
100 millilitres sweet chilli sauce
For Creamy BBQ Dip:
100 millilitres vegan mayonnaise - 50 millilitres barbecue sauce

NUTRITIONAL VALUES (PER SERVING): CALORIES: 523; CARBS: 81G; FAT: 14G; PROTEIN: 24G

Mediterranean
Vegetable Tart

🕐 **Prep:** *15 mins* 📠 **Cook:** *20 mins* 🍽 **Serves:** *4*

Directions

1. Warm up your Ninja Dual Zone Air Fryer to 200°C.
2. Score a border around your pastry rectangle. Put it onto your baking paper sheet, then transfer it to your cooking basket zone one.
3. In your big container, mix cherry tomatoes, courgette, onion, bell peppers, garlic, olive oil, vinegar, salt plus pepper.
4. Cook pastry within ten mins in zone one. Remove cooked pastry, then add vegetable mixture within your scored border.
5. Put loaded tart to your cooking basket zone one, then cook within ten mins till golden brown. Remove, cool it down, slice, then serve.

Ingredients

200 grams puff pastry, rolled out into 20cm x 30cm rectangle - 100 grams cherry tomatoes, halved - 100 grams each courgette & red onion, thinly sliced - 100 grams each yellow & red bell pepper, thinly sliced - Two cloves garlic, minced - 30 millilitres olive oil - 10 millilitres balsamic vinegar - Salt & pepper, as required

NUTRITIONAL VALUES (PER SERVING): CALORIES: 378; CARBS: 39.6G; FAT: 20.4G; PROTEIN: 6.1G

Vegan Stuffed Bell Peppers
With Quinoa

🕐 **Prep:** *15 mins* 📠 **Cook:** *30 mins* 🍽 **Serves:** *4*

Directions

1. Warm up your Ninja Dual Zone air fryer to 180°C.
2. Cook quinoa in your saucepan with stock till tender. Put aside.
3. Warm up oil in your skillet on moderate temp. Add onions, then cook within five mins till softened. Add garlic, then cook within one min.
4. Mix in cooked quinoa plus black beans. Flavour it using paprika, salt, plus pepper.
5. Put bell peppers in your baking dish, then spoon quinoa filling into each.
6. Put stuffed peppers into each cooking basket. Cook within thirty mins till peppers are tender. Serve.

Ingredients

Eight bell peppers, sliced tops & seeded - 30 millilitres olive oil - 200 grams quinoa - 150 grams onion, chopped - 10 grams garlic, minced - 200 grams black beans, strained & washed - Five grams smoked paprika - Salt & pepper, as required - 330 millilitres vegetable stock

NUTRITIONAL VALUES (PER SERVING): CALORIES: 400; CARBS: 61G; FAT: 11G; PROTEIN: 16G

Vegetarian "Fish" & Chips
With Tartar Sauce

🕐 Prep: *15* mins 📠 Cook: *25* mins 🍽 Serves: *4*

Directions

1. Warm up your Ninja Dual Zone Air Fryer to 200°C.
2. Dip each halloumi strip into flax egg mixture, then coat it in breadcrumbs.
3. Put halloumi strips in your cooking basket zone one, then cook within ten mins till golden brown, turning once.
4. In your big container, mix potato wedges, oil, salt, plus pepper.
5. Put potato wedges in your cooking basket zone two, then cook within twenty-five mins, turning often.
6. Meanwhile, mix vegan mayonnaise, pickle relish, juice, salt, plus pepper in your small container.
7. Serve both halloumi "fish" plus potato wedges with tartar sauce.

Ingredients

400 grams halloumi cheese, sliced into thick strips - 200 grams breadcrumbs - 30 millilitres ground - flaxseed mixed with water (flax egg) - 800 grams potatoes, cut into wedges - 30 millilitres vegetable oil - Salt & pepper, as required
For the Tartar Sauce:
150 millilitres vegan mayonnaise - 30 millilitres sweet pickle relish - 15 millilitres lemon juice - Salt & pepper, as required

NUTRITIONAL VALUES (PER SERVING): CALORIES: 595; CARBS: 47G; FAT: 33G; PROTEIN: 24G

Vegan Sausage & Bean
Casserole

🕐 Prep: *10* mins 📠 Cook: *20* mins 🍽 Serves: *4*

Directions

1. Warm up your Ninja Dual Zone Air Fryer to 180°C.
2. In your big container, mix sausages plus 25 millilitres oil. Put them sausages in each cooking basket, then cook within ten mins till browned, turning once.
3. In your medium pan, warm up rest of oil on moderate temp. Put onions and garlic, then cook till soft.
4. Mix in paprika, thyme, salt, plus pepper, then cook within one min. Add cherry tomatoes plus canned tomatoes, mixing well.
5. Pour in stock, then let it simmer. Add cooked sausages plus beans, then mix well.
6. Transfer casserole mixture to each cooking basket zone. Cook within ten mins till warmed. Serve.

Ingredients

400 grams vegan sausages - 800 grams tinned mixed beans, strained & washed - 200 grams cherry tomatoes, halved - 200 millilitres vegetable stock - 100 grams onions, diced - 50 millilitres olive oil - Two garlic cloves, minced - 400 grams canned chopped tomatoes - Two grams smoked paprika - One gram dried thyme - Salt & pepper, as required

NUTRITIONAL VALUES (PER SERVING): CALORIES: 525; CARBS: 60G; FAT: 20G; PROTEIN: 27G

Sweet Potato & Black Bean
Empanadas

🕐 **Prep:** *20 mins*   📱 **Cook:** *15 mins*   🍽 **Serves:** *4*

Directions

1. In your microwave-safe container, mix sweet potatoes plus water. Cook on high within five mins till sweet potatoes are soft. Strain, then mash.
2. In your big pan on moderate temp, add oil, onions, plus garlic. Cook within three mins till softened. Mix in sweet potato, beans, paprika, cumin, salt plus pepper.
3. Roll each dough into a thin circle on your floured surface. Put some sweet potato mixture onto each circle.
4. Fold dough, then press edges to seal. Warm up your Ninja Dual Zone air fryer at 190°C.
5. Put empanadas in each cooking basket zone, then cook within fifteen mins till crispy. Serve.

Ingredients

300 grams sweet potatoes, peeled & cubed - 150 grams black beans, strained & washed - 50 millilitres olive oil - 50 millilitres water - 200 grams pre-made empanada dough, split into eight - 100 grams onion, finely chopped - Two garlic cloves, minced - Five grams smoked paprika Five grams ground cumin - Salt & pepper, as required

NUTRITIONAL VALUES (PER SERVING): CALORIES: 456; CARBS: 62G; FAT: 18G; PROTEIN: 11G

Vegan Shepherd's
Pie with Lentils

🕐 **Prep:** *20 mins*   📱 **Cook:** *45 mins*   🍽 **Serves:** *4*

Directions

1. Warm up your ninja Dual Zone air fryer to 180°C. Cook potatoes in your cooking basket zone one within twenty mins till tender.
2. Meanwhile, cook green lentils in your pot with broth on moderate temp within twenty-five mins.
3. In your separate pot, warm up oil, then cook onion plus garlic on moderate temp within five mins.
4. Add mixed vegetables, then cook within ten mins till tender, mixing often.
5. Add lentils, tomatoes plus soy sauce. Mix well, then flavour it using salt plus pepper.
6. Put potatoes in your big container, then mash with almond milk till smooth.
7. Put half of lentil mixture in your casserole dish, then add mashed potatoes on top.
8. Put rest of lentil mixture on top, then cover it with mashed potatoes layer. Put casserole dish in your cooking basket zone one, then bake within twenty mins till golden-brown. Serve.

Ingredients

200 grams green lentils, dry - One kilogram mixed vegetables - One litre vegetable broth - 15 millilitres olive oil - One onion, diced - Two cloves garlic, minced - 400 grams canned chopped tomatoes - 30 millilitres soy sauce - Salt & pepper, as required - 300 grams potatoes, peeled & diced - 100 millilitres unsweetened almond milk

NUTRITIONAL VALUES (PER SERVING): CALORIES: 362; CARBS: 67G; FAT: 5G; PROTEIN: 17G

Butternut Squash
& Sage Risotto

🕐 **Prep:** *15 mins*   ▭ **Cook:** *30 mins*   🍽 **Serves:** *4*

Directions

1. Warm up your Ninja Dual Zone air fryer to 200°C.
2. In your container, mix squash cubes plus 15 millilitres oil. Transfer it onto your cooking basket zone one, then cook within fifteen mins till tender.
3. In your big saucepan, warm up rest of oil on moderate temp. Add arborio rice, then cook within two mins, mixing till lightly toasted.
4. Slowly add stock, mixing often within eighteen to twenty mins till cooked.
5. Mix in butternut squash, butter, parmesan, plus sage. Cook within two mins till warmed. Serve.

Ingredients

700 grams butternut squash, peeled & diced into 1cm cubes - 30 millilitres olive oil - One litre vegetable stock - 150 grams arborio rice - 50 grams unsalted butter - 100 grams parmesan cheese, grated - 15 sage leaves, finely chopped

NUTRITIONAL VALUES (PER SERVING): CALORIES: 490; CARBS: 60G; FAT: 21G; PROTEIN: 16G

Vegan BBQ "Pulled Pork"
Sandwiches

🕐 **Prep:** *20 mins*   ▭ **Cook:** *30 mins*   🍽 **Serves:** *4*

Directions

1. In your container, mix jackfruit plus BBQ sauce. Warm up your Ninja Dual Zone Air Fryer to 200°C.
2. Put marinated jackfruit in your greased cooking basket zone one. Cook within fifteen mins, flip jackfruit, then cook within fifteen mins till slightly crisped.
3. Mix coleslaw, mayo, apple cider, salt plus pepper in your container.
4. Put cooked jackfruit on each burger bun bottom half. Top using coleslaw, then close using rest of buns. Serve.

Ingredients

500 grams jackfruit in water, strained & shredded - 150 grams vegan BBQ sauce - 15 grams vegetable oil - 200 grams coleslaw mix - 80 grams vegan mayo - 15 millilitres apple cider vinegar - Salt & pepper, as required - Four vegan burger buns

NUTRITIONAL VALUES (PER SERVING): CALORIES 512; CARBS 68G; FAT 21G; PROTEIN 7G

Stuffed Portobello
Mushrooms with Feta

🕐 **Prep:** *10 mins*　📠 **Cook:** *15 mins*　🍽 **Serves:** *4*

Directions

1. Preheat your Ninja Dual Zone air fryer to 190°C.
2. In your container, mix feta cheese, spinach, onion, plus garlic. Flavour it using salt plus pepper. Stuff each mushroom cap with it.
3. Brush oil over stuffed mushrooms, then put them in each cooking basket zone. Cook within fifteen mins till tender. Serve.

Ingredients

Four big Portobello mushrooms, cleaned
150 grams crumbled feta cheese
100 grams chopped spinach
80 grams red onion, finely diced
6 grams garlic cloves, minced
100 millilitres olive oil
Salt & pepper, as required

NUTRITIONAL VALUES (PER SERVING): CALORIES: 342; CARBS: 10G; FAT: 30G; PROTEIN: 11G

Vegan Spinach
& "Cheese" Rolls

🕐 **Prep:** *15 mins*　📠 **Cook:** *20 mins*　🍽 **Serves:** *4*

Directions

1. Warm up your Ninja Dual Zone air fryer to 180°C.
2. In your pan, warm up oil on moderate temp. Add onion plus garlic, then cook within three mins till fragrant. Add spinach, then cook till wilted. Remove.
3. In your container, mix cream cheese, nutritional yeast, spinach mixture, salt, plus pepper.
4. Put some spinach mixture onto each puff pastry, Fold sides, then roll it up to seal. Brush each roll using water.
5. Split rolls in each basket zone, then cook within twenty mins till golden brown. Serve.

Ingredients

200 grams fresh spinach - One kilogram puff pastry, vegan, rolled out & sliced into eight rectangles - 50 millilitres olive oil - 250 grams vegan cream cheese - 100 grams nutritional yeast - 80 grams onion, chopped - Five grams garlic, minced - Salt & pepper, as required - 30 millilitres water

NUTRITIONAL VALUES (PER SERVING): CALORIES: 408; CARBS: 44G; FAT: 19G; PROTEIN: 14G

Cauliflower "Steak"
With Chimichurri Sauce

🕐 **Prep:** *10 mins*   ▣ **Cook:** *20 mins*   🍽 **Serves:** *4*

Directions

1. Warm up your Ninja Dual Zone air fryer to 200°C.
2. Brush each cauliflower steak using oil, then flavour it using salt plus pepper.
3. Put seasoned cauliflower steaks in your cooking basket sone one. Cook within ten mins, flip each steak, then cook within ten mins till tender.
4. Meanwhile, mix parsley, cilantro, garlic, vinegar, oil, pepper flakes, plus salt in your food processor. Pulse till slightly chunky.
5. Drizzle chimichurri sauce in your cauliflower steaks. Serve.

Ingredients

One big cauliflower, sliced into steaks - 30 millilitres olive oil - Salt & pepper, as required - 50 grams fresh parsley - 20 grams fresh cilantro - 6 grams garlic, minced - 60 millilitres red wine vinegar - 120 millilitres olive oil - 5 grams crushed red pepper flakes - Salt, as required

NUTRITIONAL VALUES (PER SERVING): CALORIES: 314; CARBS: 18G; FAT: 24G; PROTEIN: 7G

Vegan "Beef" Stroganoff
With Mushrooms

🕐 **Prep:** *15 mins*   ▣ **Cook:** *20 mins*   🍽 **Serves:** *4*

Directions

1. Warm up your Ninja Dual Zone Air Fryer at 200°C.
2. In your big container, mix mushrooms, vegan "beef", onion, garlic oil, salt plus pepper.
3. Add it into each cooking basket zone. Cook within fifteen mins till "beef" is warmed.
4. Meanwhile, in your medium container, mix milk, sour cream, tomato paste plus Worcestershire sauce.
5. Pour it over "beef" and mushroom mixture, then cook within five mins till creamy. Serve.

Ingredients

500 grams vegan "beef" chunks or strips - 300 grams chestnut mushrooms, sliced - 200 millilitres unsweetened almond milk - 150 grams vegan sour cream - 150 grams onion, chopped - 6 grams garlic, minced - 30 millilitres olive oil - 30 grams tomato paste - 15 millilitres vegan Worcestershire sauce - Salt & pepper, as required

NUTRITIONAL VALUES (PER SERVING): CALORIES: 375; CARBS: 18G; FAT: 25G; PROTEIN: 20G

Vegetarian Scotch
Eggs with Quorn

🕐 **Prep:** *15 mins*　📦 **Cook:** *18 mins*　🍽 **Serves:** *4*

Directions

1. Warm up your Ninja Dual Zone air fryer to 180°C.
2. In your container, mix Quorn mince, parsley, salt, plus pepper. Split it into four, then flatten each into a thin patty.
3. Roll each egg in flour, then cover it using Quorn patty.
4. Add milk in your shallow container, then put breadcrumbs in second container. Dip each Quorn-covered eggs into milk, then coat in breadcrumbs.
5. Put breaded Scotch eggs in each cooking basket zone, then cook within eighteen mins till golden brown, turning once.

Ingredients

200 grams Quorn mince
Four medium free-range eggs, boiled & peeled
100 grams wholemeal breadcrumbs
30 grams plain flour
100 millilitres milk
3.8grams fresh parsley, chopped
Salt & pepper, as required

NUTRITIONAL VALUES (PER SERVING): CALORIES: 273; CARBS: 36G; FAT: 5G; PROTEIN: 20G

Vegan Teriyaki
"Chicken" Skewers

🕐 **Prep:** *20 mins*　📦 **Cook:** *12 mins*　🍽 **Serves:** *4*

Directions

1. In your medium container, mix TVP "chicken" chunks plus half of teriyaki sauce. Marinate within ten mins.
2. In your small container, mix rest of teriyaki sauce plus cornstarch till smooth.
3. Thread marinated "chicken" chunks, bell peppers plus onion cubes onto your wooden skewers.
4. Warm up your Ninja Dual Zone Air Fryer to 200°C.
5. Put skewers in your cooking basket zone one, then cook within six mins.
6. Brush them using teriyaki-cornstarch mixture. Cook within six mins till warmed. Serve.

Ingredients

400 grams textured vegetable protein (TVP)
"chicken" chunks
120 millilitres teriyaki sauce
Nine grams cornstarch
50 grams red bell pepper, cubed
50 grams green bell pepper, cubed
50 grams red onion, cubed

NUTRITIONAL VALUES (PER SERVING): CALORIES: 310; CARBS: 45G; FAT: 4G; PROTEIN: 27G

Vegetable & Cheese
Layered Bake

🕐 **Prep:** *15 mins*   📱 **Cook:** *25 mins*   🍽 **Serves:** *4*

Directions

1. Warm up your Ninja Dual Zone Air Fryer to 180°C.
2. In your big container, mix vegetables, potatoes, oil, salt, plus pepper.
3. Split vegetable mixture in each cooking basket zone, then cook within ten mins.
4. Warm up stock in your small saucepan, then pour it over each basket.
5. Sprinkle Cheddar cheese, then cook within fifteen mins till cheese is melted.

Ingredients

500 grams mixed vegetables, sliced
200 grams potatoes, thinly sliced
150 grams Cheddar cheese, grated
100 millilitres vegetable stock
30 millilitres olive oil
Salt & pepper, as required

NUTRITIONAL VALUES (PER SERVING): CALORIES: 376; CARBS: 32G; FAT: 20G; PROTEIN: 14G

Vegan Meatball Sub
With Marinara

🕐 **Prep:** *15 mins*   📱 **Cook:** *20 mins*   🍽 **Serves:** *4*

Directions

1. Warm up your Ninja Dual Zone Air Fryer to 180°C.
2. Put vegan meatballs into each greased cooking basket zone, then cook within ten mins, turning once.
3. In your small saucepan, warm up marinara sauce on moderate-low temp. Mix in oregano, basil, salt, plus pepper.
4. Remove cooked vegan meatballs, then mix them in warmed marinara sauce. Put saucy meatballs among your four sub rolls. Sprinkle using vegan cheese.
5. Put subs back into each cooking basket, then cook within five mins till golden. Serve.

Ingredients

400 grams vegan meatballs - Four crusty sub rolls, sliced open - 200 grams vegan mozzarella cheese, shredded - 500 grams marinara sauce - 30 millilitres olive oil - 5 grams dried oregano - 5 grams dried basil - Salt & pepper, as required

NUTRITIONAL VALUES (PER SERVING): CALORIES: 550; CARBS: 65G; FAT: 20G; PROTEIN: 27G

Sticky Toffee
Pudding Cups

 **Prep:** *15 mins*    **Cook:** *25 mins*   **Serves:** *6*

Ingredients

Directions

1. In your container, mix dates, boiling water plus baking soda. Put aside within ten mins to soften.
2. In another container, cream butter plus sugar till fluffy. Put eggs, then mix till blended.
3. Fold in flour, then add milk plus vanilla till smooth. Mix in dates with their liquid.
4. Warm up your Ninja Dual Zone air fryer to 180°C. Oil six ramekins, then put batter among them.
5. Put filled ramekins into each cooking basket zone. Cook within twenty-five mins till firm.
6. Meanwhile, dissolve butter on low temp in your saucepan. Add heavy cream plus sugar, then cook while mixing often.
7. Drizzle toffee sauce on each pudding cup. Serve.

200 grams pitted dates, chopped - 250 millilitres boiling water - Five grams baking soda - 100 grams unsalted butter, softened - 100 grams light brown sugar - Two big eggs - 150 grams self-raising flour - 100 millilitres whole milk - Five millilitres pure vanilla extract

For the Toffee Sauce:
100 grams unsalted butter - 100 grams heavy cream - 150 grams light brown sugar

NUTRITIONAL VALUES (PER SERVING): CALORIES: 620; CARBS: 75G; FAT: 34G; PROTEIN: 6G

Air-Fried
Apple Pie Parcels

 **Prep:** *20 mins*    **Cook:** *15 mins*   **Serves:** *4*

Ingredients

Directions

1. In your big container, mix flour plus butter till crumbly.
2. Add cold water, then mix till a dough forms. Shape it into a ball, wrap, then chill in your fridge within ten mins.
3. Meanwhile, in your separate container, mix apples, sugar, cinnamon plus lemon juice.
4. Warm up your Ninja Dual Zone Air Fryer to 180°C.
5. Roll out chilled dough on your floured surface, then slice eight squares.
6. Spoon some apple mixture onto four dough square. Close using rest of dough.
7. Put apple pie parcels into each greased cooking basket zone. Cook within fifteen mins till crispy, turning once. Serve.

150 grams plain flour
75 grams cold unsalted butter, cubed
30 millilitres cold water
500 grams cooking apples, diced
50 grams sugar, granulated
Two grams ground cinnamon
Five millilitres lemon juice

NUTRITIONAL VALUES (PER SERVING): CALORIES 439; CARBS 68.5G; FAT 16.5G; PROTEIN 4.5G

Raspberry & White Chocolate
Muffins

🕐 **Prep:** *15 mins*   📱 **Cook:** *12 mins*   🍽 **Serves:** *6*

Directions

1. Warm up your ninja Dual Zone air fryer to 180°C.
2. In your big container, mix flour plus caster sugar.
3. In your separate container, whisk milk, egg, plus oil. Combine it with flour mixture till blended. Fold in raspberries plus white chocolate chips.
4. Split it between six muffin cases, then move them in each cooking basket zone. Cook within twelve mins till firm. Remove, cool it down, then serve.

Ingredients

200 grams flour, self-raising - 75 grams caster sugar - 100 millilitres whole milk - One big egg, beaten - 60 millilitres vegetable oil - 100 grams each fresh raspberries & white chocolate chips

NUTRITIONAL VALUES (PER SERVING): CALORIES: 324; CARBS: 45G; FAT: 12G; PROTEIN: 6G

Lemon Drizzle
Cake Slices

🕐 **Prep:** *15 mins*   📱 **Cook:** *20 mins*   🍽 **Serves:** *12*

Directions

1. Warm up your ninja Dual Zone air fryer to 180°C.
2. In your big container, cream butter plus sugar till fluffy. Add eggs, mixing well. Mix in zest. Fold in flour till blended.
3. Split it in each lined cooking basket zone, then cook within twenty mins. Remove, then cool it down.
4. Meanwhile, mix sugar plus lemon juice in your small container. Pour lemon drizzle, into cake slices. Serve.

Ingredients

225 grams flour, self-rising - 225 grams unsalted butter, softened - 225 grams sugar, granulated - Four big eggs - Zest of two lemons -

For the Lemon Drizzle:
100 grams sugar, granulated - Juice of two lemons

NUTRITIONAL VALUES (PER SERVING): CALORIES: 367; CARBS: 49G; FAT: 17G; PROTEIN: 5G

Chocolate Fondant
Puddings

🕐 **Prep:** *15 mins*   📷 **Cook:** *12 mins*   🍽 **Serves:** *4*

Directions

1. Warm up your ninja Dual Zone air fryer to 190°C.
2. In your microwave-safe container, dissolve dark chocolate plus butter till smooth.
3. In another container, whisk eggs plus sugar till fluffy. Fold in chocolate mixture till blended Mix in flour till smooth.
4. Split batter among your four greased ramekins. Put ramekins in each cooking basket zone, then cook within twelve mins till set. Cool it down.
5. Meanwhile, whip heavy cream till thick. Serve your puddings with some whipped cream.

Ingredients

200 grams dark chocolate
200 grams unsalted butter
Four big eggs
125 grams sugar, granulated
45 grams flour, all-purpose
100 millilitres heavy cream

NUTRITIONAL VALUES (PER SERVING): CALORIES: 950; CARBS: 62G; FAT: 68G; PROTEIN: 14G

Baked
Alaska Bites

🕐 **Prep:** *15 mins*   📷 **Cook:** *10 mins*   🍽 **Serves:** *6*

Directions

1. Warm up your ninja Dual Zone air fryer to 200°C.
2. Put sponge cake into each cooking basket zone. Put some ice cream on each, then freeze within five mins.
3. Meanwhile, whisk egg whites till soft peaks. Slowly whisk in caster sugar till stiff peaks form.
4. Remove your baskets, then spoon meringue on each. Put baskets your dual zone air fryer, then cook within ten mins till crispy. Serve.

Ingredients

500 grams sponge cake, cubed
500 millilitres vanilla ice cream, slightly softened
200 grams egg whites
150 grams caster sugar

NUTRITIONAL VALUES (PER SERVING): CALORIES: 386; CARBS: 65G; FAT: 9G; PROTEIN: 11G

Eton Mess
With Crispy Meringue

🕐 **Prep:** *15 mins*   🍲 **Cook:** *40 mins*   🍽 **Serves:** *4*

Directions

1. Warm up your Ninja Dual Zone Air Fryer to 100°C.
2. In your container, whisk egg whites till soft peaks. Slowly add caster sugar, whisking till glossy.
3. Spread it onto your parchment paper, making circular shape. Put parchment paper into your cooking basket zone one. Bake within forty mins till crispy.
4. Meanwhile, mix strawberries with some caster sugar in your container. Put aside within ten mins.
5. In your separate container, whip heavy cream with icing sugar plus vanilla till it forms soft peaks. Cool it down, then break it into small pieces.
6. Layer meringue, strawberry filling, plus whipped cream in your serving containers. Serve.

Ingredients

100 grams egg whites
200 grams caster sugar
300 grams strawberries, hulled & quartered
200 millilitres heavy cream
Ten grams icing sugar
Two millilitres vanilla extract

NUTRITIONAL VALUES (PER SERVING): CALORIES: 450; CARBS: 62G; FAT: 20G; PROTEIN: 5G

Banoffee Pie
In a Bowl

🕐 **Prep:** *15 mins*   🍲 **Cook:** *10 mins*   🍽 **Serves:** *4*

Directions

1. In your food processor, mix crushed biscuits plus butter till crumbly.
2. Divide it between four containers, pressing down. Chill in your fridge within ten mins.
3. Whip double cream in your container till it forms soft peaks. Fold in dulce de leche.
4. Remove prepared containers, then split whipped cream mixture between each. Put banana slices on top.
5. Warm up your Ninja Dual Zone Air Fryer to 180°C.
6. Spread dark chocolate on your parchment paper, then put it in your cooking basket zone one. Cook within two mins till dissolved. Drizzle it on each Banoffee Pie, then serve.

Ingredients

200 grams digestive biscuits, crushed
75 grams unsalted butter, melted
300 millilitres double cream
150 grams dulce de leche or caramel sauce
Two bananas, sliced
50 grams dark chocolate, grated

NUTRITIONAL VALUES (PER SERVING): CALORIES: 625; CARBS: 62G; FAT: 39G; PROTEIN: 6G

Churros
With Chocolate Sauce

🕐 **Prep:** *15 mins*   📮 **Cook:** *10 mins*   🍽 **Serves:** *4*

Directions

1. In your medium saucepan, mix water, butter, plus salt. Warm it up on moderate temp till dissolved.
2. Add flour, then mix well till a smooth dough form. Remove, then cool it down. Add eggs, mixing till glossy.
3. Warm up your Ninja Dual Zone Air Fryer to 180°C.
4. Transfer churro dough into your piping bag. Pipe churros onto your lined tray, then spray them using oil spray.
5. Move it in each cooking basket zone. Cook within ten mins, turning once,
6. Meanwhile, warm up double cream in your small saucepan on low temp till steaming.
7. Pour it on chocolate, then let it sit within one min till smooth. Mix cooked churros in sugar-cinnamon mixture, then serve with chocolate sauce.

Ingredients

**200 grams flour, all-purpose - 250 millilitres water - 50 grams unsalted butter - One gram salt
Two big eggs - 50 grams granulated sugar mixed with two grams cinnamon, ground (for coating)**

**For the chocolate sauce:
100 grams dark chocolate, chopped -
150 millilitres double cream**

NUTRITIONAL VALUES (PER SERVING): CALORIES: 562; CARBS: 57G; FAT: 33G; PROTEIN: 11G

Black Forest
Cake Pops

🕐 **Prep:** *20 mins*   📮 **Cook:** *10 mins*   🍽 **Serves:** *6*

Directions

1. In your container, mix crumbled cake, cream cheese, cherry preserve, plus vanilla till a dough form.
2. Shape it into twelve cake balls, then put them on your lined tray. Refrigerate within thirty mins.
3. Dissolve dark chocolate in your microwave-safe container at thirty-second intervals, mixing till smooth.
4. Dip each cake ball into dark chocolate. Put them back onto your tray, then let it set.
5. Dissolve white chocolate just like you did with dark chocolate, then drizzle it cake pops.
6. Warm up your Ninja Dual Zone Air Fryer to 160°C. Put coated cake pops in each cooking basket zone, then cook within ten mins till slightly crisp.

Ingredients

**200 grams chocolate sponge cake, crumbled
100 grams cream cheese
50 grams cherry preserve
100 grams dark chocolate
Two millilitres vanilla extract
150 grams white chocolate**

NUTRITIONAL VALUES (PER SERVING): CALORIES: 450; CARBS: 52G; FAT: 25G; PROTEIN: 5G

Crispy Bread
& Butter Pudding

🕐 **Prep:** *15* mins   ⏲ **Cook:** *25* mins   🍽 **Serves:** *6*

Directions

1. Warm up your ninja Dual Zone Air Fryer to 160°C.
2. Spread butter on your bread slices, then slice them into quarters.
3. Layer buttered bread pieces in your baking dish, then sprinkle it using raisins plus sultanas.
4. In your container, whisk milk, double cream, eggs, sugar, plus vanilla.
5. Pour it on bread layers, then put baking dish in your cooking basket zone on, mixing well. Cook within twenty-five mins till crispy. Serve.

Ingredients

250 grams day-old bread, sliced - 100 grams unsalted butter, softened - 75 grams raisins - 75 grams sultanas - 150 millilitres whole milk - 150 millilitres double cream - Three big eggs - 100 grams sugar, granulated - Two millilitres vanilla extract

NUTRITIONAL VALUES (PER SERVING): CALORIES: 534; CARBS: 60G; FAT: 28G; PROTEIN: 11G

Orange & Polenta
Cake

🕐 **Prep:** *20* mins   ⏲ **Cook:** *40* mins   🍽 **Serves:** *8*

Directions

1. Warm up your ninja Dual Zone Air Fryer to 160°C.
2. In your big container, cream butter plus sugar till fluffy. Add ground almonds, polenta, juice, plus zest, then mix well.
3. Beat in eggs, mixing well. Mix in vanilla, baking powder, plus salt till blended.
4. Pour it into your greased baking dish, then move it in your cooking basket zone one. Cook within forty mins till firm. Remove, cool it down, then serve.

Ingredients

200 grams unsalted butter, softened - 200 grams granulated sugar - 150 grams ground almonds - 150 grams instant polenta - Two big oranges, juice & zest - Four medium eggs - Seven millilitres vanilla extract - Five grams baking powder - Salt, as required

NUTRITIONAL VALUES (PER SERVING): CALORIES: 470; CARBS: 40G; FAT: 30G; PROTEIN: 8G

Mini Pavlovas
With Mixed Berries

🕐 **Prep:** *15 mins*   ▣ **Cook:** *20 mins*   🍽 **Serves:** *4*

Directions

1. Warm up your Ninja Dual Zone Air Fryer to 150°C.
2. In your container, whisk egg whites till stiff peaks. Add caster sugar, while whisking till thick.
3. Put four meringue mixture portions onto your warm lined baking tray.
4. Put tray in your cooking basket zone one, then cook within twenty mins till crispy. Cool them down.
5. Meanwhile, mix berries plus juice in your container. Top each pavlova with whipped cream plus berries, then lightly dust with icing sugar. Serve.

Ingredients

100 grams caster sugar
Two big egg whites
300 millilitres whipped cream
200 grams mixed berries
10 millilitres lemon juice
10 grams icing sugar

NUTRITIONAL VALUES (PER SERVING): CALORIES: 298; CARBS: 39G; FAT: 14G; PROTEIN: 4G

Dark Chocolate & Mint
Profiteroles

🕐 **Prep:** *20 mins*   ▣ **Cook:** *15 mins*   🍽 **Serves:** *6*

Directions

1. In your medium saucepan, mix butter plus water on moderate temp. Once boiling, remove your saucepan, then add flour, mixing till smooth. Cool it down, then whisk in eggs.
2. Warm up your Ninja Dual Zone Air Fryer to 180°C.
3. Spoon some batter onto each cooking basket zone. Cook within fifteen mins till golden. Remove them, then cool it down.
4. Meanwhile, whisk cream plus sugar till soft peaks, then refrigerate briefly.
5. Dissolve dark chocolate in your heatproof container on your pan with simmering water. Add mint extract, then mix well.
6. Fill each profiterole using whipped cream filling, then drizzle chocolate-mint mixture on top. Serve.

Ingredients

75 grams plain flour - 50 grams unsalted butter
- 240 millilitres water - Three eggs - 200 grams
dark chocolate - 100 millilitres mint extract

For the Filling:
300 millilitres whipping cream - 50 grams caster
sugar

NUTRITIONAL VALUES (PER SERVING): CALORIES: 650; CARBS: 60G; FAT: 41G; PROTEIN: 12G

Treacle Tart with
Clotted Cream

🕐 **Prep:** *20 mins*   ☐ **Cook:** *30 mins*   🍽 **Serves:** *8*

Directions

1. In your big container, mix flour, butter, plus sugar till crumbly.
2. pour ice-cold water, then mix till a dough forms. Wrap, then chill in your fridge within fifteen mins.
3. Warm up your Ninja Dual Zone air fryer to 180°C.
4. Roll out chilled dough on your floured surface, then press it into your tart tin.
5. In your separate container, mix golden syrup, breadcrumbs, plus zest. Pour it into your tart shell.
6. Put filled tart in each cooking basket zone, then cook within thirty mins till crust is golden. Remove, cool it down, then slice into eight.
7. Serve each with clotted cream on top.

Ingredients

300 grams flour, all-purpose - 150 grams unsalted butter, chilled & sliced into small cubes - 100 grams sugar, granulated - 50 millilitres ice-cold water - 500 grams golden syrup - 100 grams fresh breadcrumbs - Two lemons, zested - 150 millilitres clotted cream

NUTRITIONAL VALUES (PER SERVING): CALORIES: 630; CARBS: 100G; FAT: 24G; PROTEIN: 6G

Strawberry & Cream
Tartlets

🕐 **Prep:** *20 mins*   ☐ **Cook:** *10 mins*   🍽 **Serves:** *4*

Directions

1. In your big container, mix flour plus butter till crumbly.
2. Slowly add ice-cold water, then mix till a dough forms. Knead it, wrap, then refrigerate within thirty mins.
3. Warm up your Ninja Dual Zone Air Fryer to 180°C.
4. Split chilled dough into four, then roll them out in your tartlet tins.
5. Put tartlet tins into each cooking basket zone, then cook within ten mins till golden. Remove, then cool it down.
6. Meanwhile, mix mascarpone, double cream, icing sugar, plus vanilla in your container. Fill each tartlet with it. Top each filled tartlet using strawberry, then serve.

Ingredients

200 grams flour, all-purpose - 100 grams cold unsalted butter, cubed - 50 millilitres ice-cold water - 300 grams strawberries, hulled & halved - 150 grams mascarpone cheese - 100 millilitres double cream - 50 grams icing sugar - 1.5 grams vanilla extract

NUTRITIONAL VALUES (PER SERVING): CALORIES: 648; CARBS: 58G; FAT: 41G; PROTEIN: 10G

Custard-Filled
Doughnuts

🕐 **Prep:** *30 mins*　📟 **Cook:** *10 mins*　🛎 **Serves:** *8*

Directions

1. In your big container, mix flour, dry yeast, caster sugar, plus salt. Add milk, egg, plus butter, then mix well till you have a dough.
2. Cover, then let it rest within one hour till doubled in size. Transfer it to your lightly floured surface, roll it out, then slice out eight circles.
3. Warm up your Ninja Dual Zone Air Fryer to 180°C.
4. Put dough circles on each cooking basket zone. Cook within five mins per side till golden. Remove, then cool it down.
5. Make a small hole on each doughnut, then pipe it using custard. Dust your doughnuts using icing sugar, then serve.

Ingredients

250 grams plain flour - Seven grams dry yeast - 30 grams caster sugar - 120 millilitres warm milk - One big egg, beaten - 30 grams unsalted butter, dissolved - Salt, as required - 200 grams store-bought custard - Icing sugar, for dusting

---

NUTRITIONAL VALUES (PER SERVING): CALORIES: 280; CARBS: 45G; FAT: 8G; PROTEIN: 6G

Rhubarb & Custard
Crumbles

🕐 **Prep:** *15 mins*　📟 **Cook:** *30 mins*　🛎 **Serves:** *4*

Directions

1. Warm up your Ninja Dual Zone Air Fryer to 180°C.
2. In your big container, mix rhubarb pieces plus 50 grams caster sugar. Split it among four ramekins.
3. In another container, mix flour plus rest of caster sugar. Add butter, then mix well till crumbly. Mix in oats.
4. Put crumble topping on each ramekin, then move them in each cooking basket zone.
5. Cook within thirty mins, till rhubarb is tender. Remove, then cool it down. Serve it with custard on top.

Ingredients

400 grams rhubarb, trimmed & sliced into 2cm pieces - 80 grams caster sugar - 125 grams plain flour - 75 grams unsalted butter, chilled & diced - 50 grams rolled oats - One litre ready-made custard, warmed

---

NUTRITIONAL VALUES (PER SERVING): CALORIES 505; CARBS 80G; FAT 18G; PROTEIN 8G

Air-Fried
Cinnamon Rolls

🕐 **Prep:** *20 mins*   ▣ **Cook:** *8 mins*   🍽 **Serves:** *6*

Directions

1. Warm up your Ninja Dual Zone Air Fryer to 180°C.
2. In your big container, mix flour, yeast, salt, plus caster sugar. Add warm milk, butter, plus egg till you have a dough. Knead it within ten mins till elastic.
3. Roll out dough into a 30cmx20cm rectangle. Put butter onto your dough, then sprinkle brown sugar plus cinnamon powder on top.
4. Roll up your dough from its longer side, then slice into six. Put cinnamon rolls into each cooking basket zone. Cook within eight mins till golden brown.
5. Meanwhile, mix icing sugar plus milk in your small container till smooth. Remove cinnamon rolls, then cool them down. Drizzle it using glaze, then serve.

Ingredients

300 grams flour, all-purpose - 5 grams active dry yeast - 120 millilitres warm milk - Two grams salt - 60 grams caster sugar - 40 grams unsalted butter, dissolved - One medium egg
For the filling:
60 grams softened butter - 50 grams soft brown sugar - 10 grams cinnamon powder
For the glaze:
100 grams icing sugar - 30 millilitres milk

NUTRITIONAL VALUES (PER SERVING): CALORIES: 436; CARBS: 75G; FAT: 13G; PROTEIN: 8G

Victoria Sponge
With Raspberry Jam

🕐 **Prep:** *20 mins*   ▣ **Cook:** *16 mins*   🍽 **Serves:** *8*

Directions

1. Warm up your Ninja Dual Zone Air Fryer to 180°C.
2. In your big container, mix flour, caster sugar, plus butter. Add eggs plus vanilla, then mix well. Slowly pour milk, then mix well till smooth.
3. Split batter into each lined cooking basket zone, then cook within eight mins till firm. Remove, then cool them down.
4. Spread some raspberry jam on one sponge cake, then cover using rest of sponge cake. Serve.

Ingredients

250 grams flour, self-raising
250 grams caster sugar
250 grams unsalted butter, softened
Four big eggs
5 millilitres vanilla extract
50 millilitres milk
200 grams raspberry jam

NUTRITIONAL VALUES (PER SERVING): CALORIES: 535; CARBS: 55G; FAT: 33G; PROTEIN: 9G

Conclusion

With "**SUPER EASY DUAL ZONE AIR FRYER COOKBOOK UK,**" you have a variety of delicious and healthy snacks recipes which will definitely take you to another level in cooking. We believe that as you have moved through the different chapters, seeing some of these wonderful recipes and ideas, you feel ready to start using your Ninja Dual Zone Air Fryer in everyday cooking using unconventional options.

Finally, don't forget to have fun and explore different dishes once in a while. Nothing replaces practice, so you should cook as much as possible, exploring all types of cooking styles and cuisines. Your Ninja Dual Zone Air Fryer, too, can be very flexible; make sure that it remains a necessary addition to a new kitchen where you play around with different types of foods and meals.

Remember to always put your safety first while maintaining good cleaning habits on your air fryer for longevity as well as perfect outcomes. Refresh yourself with the basics of air frying like what to set as the temperatures and how to arrange your food in the side-by-side chambers.

Try using this ground-breaking appliance in your everyday meals or weekend treats for a change. Eating healthily does not mean you should have tasteless meals. With you ninja dual zone air fry, every meal you take is sumptuous yet healthy.

Finally, enjoy this culinary journey! Bring happiness by sharing homemade, healthy dishes, cooked in the spirit and care for deliciousness. Invite your family members over for a tasty meal when you are comfortable enough to share your skills.

HERE IS YOUR FREE GIFT!

- 30 GLOBAL FLAVOURS RECIPES

- 30-DAY MEAL PLAN

- WEEKLY SHOPPING LIST

SCAN HERE TO DOWNLOAD IT

Printed in Great Britain
by Amazon